DIARY OF A ROCK AND ROLL TOUR MANAGER

DIARY OF A ROCK AND ROLL TOUR MANAGER

2,190 DAYS AND NIGHTS WITH THE SOUTH'S PREMIER ROCK BAND

WILLIE PERKINS

MERCER UNIVERISTY PRESS
MACON, GEORIGA

MUP/P645

Mercer University Press
1501 Mercer University Drive
Macon, Georgia 31207
www.mupress.org

26 25 24 23 22 5 4 3 2 1

The paper used in this publication meets the minimum requirements of American National Standards for Information Science—Permanence of Paper for Printed Library Materials, ANSI Z39.48–1984.

Cataloging-in-Publication Data on file at the Library of Congress

Printed in the U.S.A.
Book design by Burt&Burt
The interior is set in Meta Serif Pro and Gill Sans Nova

ISBN 978-0-88146-846-5

Printed in the United States.

TO LINDA FLORES

PREFACE

Between June 1970 and June 1976, as tour manager for The Allman Brothers Band, I worked literally hundreds of concert tour dates and also worked with the band on a daily basis when they were not on tour. What follows is a chronicle of some of that history.

Willie Perkins
Macon, Georgia

INTRODUCTION

What exactly does a rock and roll tour manager do? Short answer: virtually everything related to the band's well-being, comfort, and performances on the road other than actually playing and singing.

From the moment a band accepts a proposed performance engagement from their personal manager and booking agent, the tour manager steps in to plan and execute all logistical coordination necessary to transport; house; supervise setup of sound, lights, and equipment; compute and collect all contractual performance monies due the band; pay all expenses related to the performance, including payroll; and collect and retain all records and receipts for bookkeeping, auditing, and tax purposes. Tours usually consisted of multiple dates in multiple cities for weeks or even months of time on the road away from home.

Back in the late 1960s, I had met and become a casual friend and devoted fan of The Allman Brothers Band, a virtually unknown young rock band from the South, through their then tour manager, Twiggs Lyndon, a longtime close friend of mine. I was working as an auditor and fraud investigator for a large Atlanta bank but wanted to quit and become a member of the band's road crew. I had a feeling their amazing talent would propel them to the pinnacle of success and wanted to help them in any way possible. I had asked Twiggs to consider me for the first available job opening, and he promised he would. Who could have guessed it would be his? Little did I know what a long, amazing ride it would be. Let's hit the road!

Willie Perkins
Macon, Georgia

1970

APRIL 29, 1970

ALIOTTA'S LOUNGE

BUFFALO, NEW YORK

The Allman Brothers Band, a young, virtually unknown rock band from the South, played what was ostensibly a routine club date in Buffalo, New York. My good friend Twiggs Lyndon was their tour manager. Twiggs was a seasoned veteran of the road, having toured with Little Richard, Percy Sledge, Sam and Dave, Otis Redding, Arthur Conley, and others.

There is one almost undisputed rule in rock and roll that is rarely broken: the band must be paid in full the day of the show. It was a bad omen when the band's $500 payment was delayed until the following day. The next morning, club owner Angelo Aliotta once again gave Twiggs the runaround. An argument and fight ensued, and Twiggs fatally stabbed Mr. Aliotta. A very fatigued and stressed Twiggs had acted upon his sense of honor and allegiance to the band and was charged with first-degree murder. In a nonjury trial before a judge, John Condon, a highly skilled local attorney hired by the band, was able to get a verdict of not guilty by reason of insanity. The stress of the job and resultant drug use played a huge role in the verdict. I was told the Aliotta family initially sought physical retribution against Twiggs, but the local mafia don forbade it because he judged it was a legitimate debt that should have been paid. Twiggs was confined to a mental institution where his condition greatly improved. He was subsequently released in about a year and rejoined the band as stage manager.

I had previously expressed great interest in joining the band crew, and Twiggs had told me the next opening would be mine, but no one could have imagined these tragic circumstances. Would I get a call from the band?

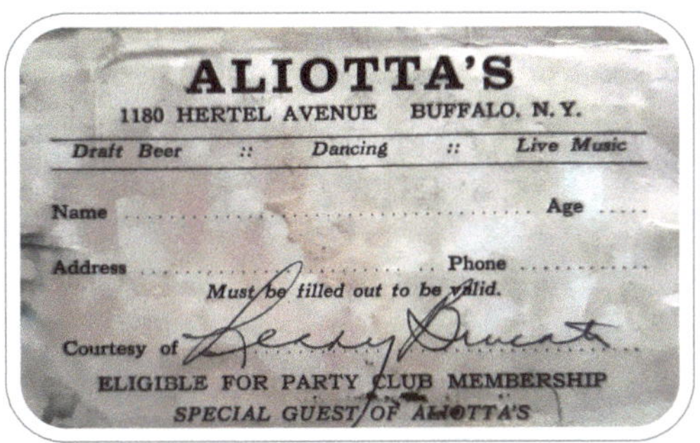
ALIOTTA'S
1180 HERTEL AVENUE BUFFALO, N.Y.
Draft Beer :: Dancing :: Live Music
Name .... Age .....
Address .... Phone ....
Must be filled out to be valid.
Courtesy of ....
ELIGIBLE FOR PARTY CLUB MEMBERSHIP
SPECIAL GUEST OF ALIOTTA'S

MAY 1, 1970

ALLEN THEATRE

CLEVELAND

The band was billed second to the Youngbloods. NRBQ opened. It was a sad trip south without Twiggs, who remained in Buffalo's Erie County Jail, Cell J-2. I would visit Twiggs once and correspond with him often in the months to come.

That day, I received a phone call from band member Butch Trucks, who told me that Twiggs had recommended me to replace him as tour manager. No one could really replace Twiggs at any task, and I only had a vague understanding of the job duties and responsibilities, but I was willing to give it a try. I really felt this band was going to be hugely successful, and I wanted to be a part of it. Butch suggested I meet with them at their Atlanta show at Georgia Tech on May 9, and I agreed to be there. Both the band and I had a big decision to make.

MAY 9, 1970

GEORGIA TECH

ALEXANDER MEMORIAL COLISEUM, ATLANTA

The band received $2,000 to open the show for headliner Smith, which was big money for them at this stage of their career. Experienced booking agents knew to request high prices when they negotiated with colleges and universities since most usually had plenty of discretionary funds in their student activities accounts. A student advisory board was usually given wide latitude in who they selected and what they paid without much interference from the school administration. They usually accepted the first offer tendered by the band's booking agent.

After the show, Duane Allman and I sat down face-to-face in a booth in the lounge of the band's Winnebago camper that they toured in. He explained to me the complexity of the tour manager's job, with its myriad responsibilities and the extreme stress and long hours involved. He emphasized how difficult and demanding it would be to execute my duties while dealing with the complex and often temperamental personalities of the nine members of the band and crew.

Duane offered me the job based on Twiggs's recommendation, and I accepted. My starting date would be June 1, and I would be paid a ninety-dollar weekly salary, the same as all band and crew members received at that time. If there was not enough cash on hand to make payroll, the crew would be paid first equally from whatever funds were available. That was Duane's rule. Twiggs had been paid an additional fifty dollars weekly by manager Phil Walden's office, and I would receive that also. For a while, I was the highest paid member of the entire organization. Duane and the other band members approved this because they felt the tour manager's position deserved it. I was determined not to disappoint their confidence in me.

JUNE 2, 1970

GOULD AUDITORIUM

JEKYLL ISLAND, GEORGIA

This was my first official gig. It was a high school seniors graduation party, and the fee was $1,000. In retrospect, I salute whoever was responsible for having the wisdom and perception to select the virtually unknown Allman Brothers Band for their event. I am sure it has become a conversation piece over the years.

Normally, the band and crew would travel together, caravanning from Macon in the Winnebago camper and an old Dodge equipment truck, a retired Avis rental unit with a slant six-cylinder engine that would deliver thousands of heavy-duty miles from coast to coast. Eventually, both it and the Winnebago would expire from exhaustion. Bless those old vehicles!

NATIONAL 45-104 EYE-EASE 45-404 20-20 BUFF MADE IN U.S.A.

June 2, 1970 Gould Auditorium
Jekyll Island, Georgia

E. A. Martin, Chief Promotions $1,000.00 less $350.00 deposit = 650.00 pickup

		1	2	3	4
Travel	Cash Advance	$ 20000			
	Pickup	65000			
	Equipment Crew Expense		$ 5000		
	Gasoline - Group		4519		
	Misc Food & Beverage		2600		
	Currency		7800		
	Coin		81		
	Checks		65000		
		$ 85000	$ 85000		
	Deposit 6-4-70				
	General Account				
	Currency	$ 7800			
	Coin	81			
	Checks	65000			
		$ 72881			

cwf

Logistics were rarely without complications, as I would soon learn. On this occasion, the band had been working in Florida, so I would meet them on Jekyll. I was accompanied by Earl "Speedo" Simms, former tour manager for Otis Redding, whom the band's management had sent out to walk me through that first gig. He impressed upon me the importance of keeping complete control of the tour manager's briefcase that I inherited from Twiggs. It contained all the cash, contracts, receipts, and records. Remember, there were no laptops, internet, or cell phones. The whole operation was dependent on public and motel phones, that briefcase, and my brain. Thankfully, none ever failed. The Allman Brothers Band never missed a show except for rare, severe cases of illness, and they never, ever failed to get paid in full.

That first show went smoothly. Speedo returned to Macon and I was on my own. It was rumored there was an "over and under" betting pool back at the Walden management office on how many days I would last. As it turned out, quite a few. If you bet on the "over," you won. Let the adventure begin!

JUNE 11, 1970

NORT'S LASCENE

COCOA BEACH, FLORIDA

Nort's LaScene in Cocoa Beach, Florida, was a nightclub/disco that sometimes featured live bands. Shows in bars, nightclubs, and discos were referred to as "club dates." Clubs could be one-room, barn-like buildings or ornate glass-and-chrome structures that would feel right at home in Las Vegas. They all had one thing in common: clouds of smoke from cigarettes and other sources and sticky floors from who knows what. Most had, if any, tiny, filthy dressing rooms. As wrestler Jerry Lawler has said, "You could put a wash rag on the floor and have wall-to-wall carpeting." As I recall, the club dressing room was the club office, and owner, Nort, paid me right out of the office safe.

The Allman Brothers Band had some of their best performances in clubs and would play many of them in their first two years of touring.

JUNE 13, 1970

ATLANTA STADIUM

ATLANTA

My first big outdoor stadium event was the Cosmic Carnival featuring Traffic, Ten Years After, Frank Zappa, Ike and Tina Turner, It's a Beautiful Day, Albert King, Mountain, The Allman Brothers Band, and others. Such a line up could not miss, right? Wrong. The stadium was the home of the Atlanta Braves and Atlanta Falcons, and that was part of the problem. No concertgoers were allowed on the field and were seated in hard stadium chairs far from the stage (which was at the second-base position). This and other problems kept the attendance much lower than anticipated. Many bands were not going to be paid in full or at all and refused to perform, which disappointed the attendees even more.

The Allman Brothers Band management representative, Bunky Odom, and I met the promoter, Forrest Hamilton, in the Braves dugout and agreed on a renegotiated fee, which we received. Mr. Hamilton begged me to notify Duane to please not invite the fans down on the field to avoid a police shutdown. Of course, Duane did invite the fans down before I could reach him. They poured onto the field and the concert was briefly stopped before order was restored and they returned to their seats. Duane, aware of the bad vibes, invited everyone to a free concert in Atlanta's Piedmont Park the following afternoon. No plans or permits had been secured for this, but we did it anyway without any repercussions.

In June 1974, the band would return to Atlanta Stadium to perform before 61,232 fans, with seating allowed on the field but even more drama. That time, they would be paid more than one hundred times what they earned in 1970.

MOUNTAIN

Mountain is a four-piece rock group that plays hard and heavy. The group features Felix Pappulardi who gave us the Cream on bass. On guitar is Leslie West, known to many from Forest Hills and Bayside as Leslie Weinstein. Leslie was the lead guitarist for the Vagrents a few years back but an accident which spelled disaster for the Action House did the same for the Famous N. Y. Group. The other members of the group are N. D. Smart II on drums and N. Lansbery on the organ.

TRAFFIC

Traffic was one of the first creative Rock Groups to come from England. Living and creative in a small country cottage in Berkshire they developed a style of their own. Steve Winwood, Chris Wood, and Jim Cipaldi make up the group
The group broke up 1 year ago but have reformed minus Dave Mason.

Ike & Tina Turner

Ike & Tina are a combination of R & B and genius. Tina's completely feminine blues voice highlights the driving rythms of Ike. They have been around thrilling audiences for a long time, but it is only recently that they have received the recognition they deserve. They appeared with the Stones on their recent U.S. Tour and proved that they are one of the top blues acts in the country.

SWEETWATER

ALLMAN BROTHERS

With Duane Allman (lead guitarand vocals), Greg Allman (organ and vocals), Butch Truchs and Jai Johanny Johnson (drummers), Dick Betts (guitar), and Berry Oakley (bass) the band has emerged from the chrysalis of their active hibernation with their music free of cliches.

JULY 3–5, 1970

MIDDLE GEORGIA RACEWAY

BYRON, GEORGIA

The second Atlanta Pop Festival was held at a racetrack set amid pecan groves in Byron, Georgia, just southwest of Macon. Performers included The Allman Brothers Band, Cactus, the Chambers Brothers, Grand Funk Railroad, Richie Havens, Jimi Hendrix, B. B. King, It's a Beautiful Day, and many others. Some other advertised acts did not perform.

The Allman Brothers Band was to open and close the show as unofficial hosts. Early on, the fans had overwhelmed the entrance gates, and the festival was declared "free" to the delight of those who had not purchased tickets. Crowd size estimates ranged from one hundred thousand to more than three hundred thousand. The temperature exceeded 100 degrees, and there was rampant drug use and nudity, but all survived in peace and love.

Duane had been recording in Miami, but he assured me he would drive up and arrive on time. As showtime approached, Duane had not arrived, and I was nervously pacing at the performer's entrance when he casually rode up on the back of a stranger's motorcycle. His car had been hopelessly tied up in traffic south of the venue, and he abandoned it to hop a ride on the cycle. We would retrieve his car the following week.

So, the Brothers opened the show on time and would close it in the predawn hours of Monday morning. It was obvious there would be no cash to pay the bands, but we were not going to walk out on this historic hometown event. Promoter Alex Cooley paid me with a check, normally a no-no. It was

INTERNATIONAL VENTURES, INC.
PRESENTS THE SECOND ANNUAL
ATLANTA INTERNATIONAL POP FESTIVAL
GATE SALE
Est. Price $6.79
State Tax .21
TOTAL $7.00
FRIDAY
JULY
3
—1970—
MIDDLE GEORGIA RACEWAY
• BRYON EXIT I-75 SOUTH •
003004
SECOND ANNUAL
ATLANTA INTERNATIONAL
POP FESTIVAL
MIDDLE GEORGIA
RACEWAY
GATE SALE
Total Adm. $7.00 Tax Incl.
ADMIT ONE
Good Only
FRIDAY
JULY
3
1970
VOID IF DETACHED
003004

drawn on the Atlanta bank where I had worked, so exhausted, but hopeful, I raced to Atlanta Monday morning and cashed it while there were still enough funds available to cover it. Others were not so fortunate, but Alex Cooley was an honorable man and eventually paid all his debts from the festival.

Postscript: the entire festival was professionally filmed for release as a feature motion picture, but only the Hendrix footage has ever been commercially released. I have seen it all, and if you watch carefully you can see Duane playing slide in one segment with the broken neck of a Heineken beer bottle, as he had misplaced his usual Coricidin cold-medicine bottle.

JULY 10, 1970

SUNY STONY BROOK

STONY BROOK, NEW YORK

SUNY stands for State University of New York. There are several individual campuses throughout the state, and we played concerts at many of them. By far the favorite was the Stony Brook campus located on Long Island's north shore east of New York City. A particularly hip musical environment existed there, and The Allman Brothers Band was becoming a huge favorite among the students. We would play there many times, and some excellent concert recordings exist. At this booking, the band opened for Leslie West and Mountain, but most felt The Allman Brothers Band stole the show. This happened often when they opened for better-recognized artists. Concertgoers in the Northeast were quickly becoming aware of the band and beginning a love affair with what they heard and saw.

JULY 17–19, 1970

LOVE VALLEY FESTIVAL

LOVE VALLEY, NORTH CAROLINA

The Love Valley Festival was held in the Love Valley community near Statesville, North Carolina, just north of Charlotte. It was one of the last rock festivals that could be deemed a success. Large outdoor multiday events were fast becoming extinct because the crowds were unmanageable, local officials were denying permits, and promoters were unwilling to take the large financial risks. Along with The Allman Brothers Band, acts included Wet Willie, Big Brother, Tony Joe White, Johnny Jenkins, Hampton Grease Band, and other regional bands. Crowd estimates ranged from seventy-five thousand to two hundred thousand. Approximately twenty-five thousand tickets had been sold in advance, but thousands more would swarm the location.

Love Valley was a unique, idyllic location with an Old West town motif. It had one unpaved street with stores on both sides ending in a natural outdoor amphitheater where rodeos were held. This became the concert site. Horseback riders and pedestrians were allowed, but no automobiles. I can recall looking out from the stage over the crowd and seeing what looked like hundreds of hippie encampments in the vast woods beyond. Some excellent films and photos of the event remain in circulation today.

Andy Barker was the founder and mayor of Love Valley. He presided over the town with his wife, Ellenora, and children, son Jet and daughter Tonda. I believe only the daughter survives today. Jet and Tonda were instrumental in getting Andy to promote the event. We became great friends with the family and visited them many times for brief respites from the road, including one time when our Winnebago camper broke down returning to Macon, and another when a festival up North was cancelled as we traveled. Dickey Betts even lived there briefly in a remote cabin with no phone. I would call son Jet to hand deliver messages to Dickey on horseback.

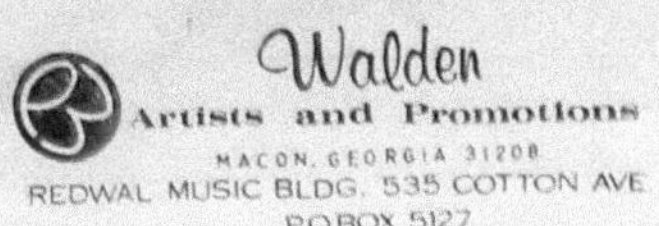

Booking Slip

DATE ISSUED 7/6/70

DATE DUE Complete in Office

EMPLOYEE(S) Allman Brothers Band

LEADER Duane Allman

TO CONSIST OF 6

DATE(S) OF ENGAGEMENT July 18 & 19

TERMS $3250.00

DEPOSIT $2769.65 (Rec.)

HOURS OF EMPLOYMENT 1 Show between 12.00 Midnight & 2 AM

REHEARSAL

LOCATION Love Valley

STREET

CITY/STATE Love Valley, N.C.

TELEPHONE(S)

CONTRACT NO. AFM ~~#225~~ #250

AFM ☒ AGVA ☐ OTHER ☐

ANOTHER AGENCY ☐ Andy Barker

EMPLOYER(S) Love Valley

STREET C/O Mayor's Office

CITY/STATE Love Valley, N.C.

TELEPHONES (704) 592-2426

COMMISSIONS DUE OFFICE

COMMISSIONS DUE EMPLOYEE

CHARGES

SEND PUBLICITY WITH CONTRACT ☐

HOLD PUBLICITY FOR CONTRACT ☐

SPECIAL INSTRUCTIONS:

D.P. 7/15

Rec. 1,039.65 7/15/70 W.U. Money Order

JULY 26, 1970

SUNY STONY BROOK

STONY BROOK, NEW YORK

I describe in an earlier section how students on campus activities boards often booked the bands that played at their schools. It was unheard of for a national act to play a college more than once every few years at the most. The relationship between the students at Stony Brook and The Allman Brothers Band, however, was a very special one and highly unusual to say the least. Not only had the band played there twice already, in April and July of 1970, we were returning for a third appearance barely three weeks later! The Allman Brothers Band had truly become such a favorite there that they could be called the unofficial "house band" on campus, and we returned again for a fourth concert in October of that year.

AUGUST 12, 1970

THE SPECTRUM

PHILADELPHIA

The Spectrum was a large indoor sports and entertainment venue with a capacity of about eighteen thousand for concerts. It opened in the fall of 1967 and was demolished beginning in November 2010. Concerts were promoted by Electric Factory Concerts, founded in 1968 by Larry Magid and the Spivak brothers, Jerry, Allen, and Herbert. It was named after their original concert venue, which was located in an old tire-company building. They promoted more than 2,500 concerts through the years before selling the company in 2008.

Three bands performed at this show, and The Allman Brothers Band played second, prior to headliner Chicago. The band would eventually headline there many times, earning huge paydays. The only thing I didn't like about the Spectrum was that their box office always withheld a tiny percentage of the band's fee for City of Philadelphia Income Tax. There was no way to avoid it without spending more than the amount withheld.

AUGUST 22, 1970

THE WAREHOUSE

NEW ORLEANS

The Warehouse, as it is commonly known, was an old cotton warehouse on Tchoupitoulas Street with a capacity of about 3,500. It was the city's premier rock concert venue in the 1970s and 1980s, and The Allman Brothers Band was a huge favorite there. The band eventually headlined at the Warehouse many times, especially on New Year's Eve shows.

On this visit, the promoters advised us that the band the Ides of March was contractually mandated to close the show, primarily because of their current number-two smash hit single "Vehicle." That was fine with The Allman Brothers Band. After their blistering set, few in the audience cared about hearing the Ides of March play the song "Vehicle" or anything else.

The Warehouse remained the premier rock venue in New Orleans from its opening in 1970 to its closing in 1982. It was razed in 1989. Interestingly, a wooden ceiling beam purchased at the demolition is housed at The Allman Brothers Band Museum at the Big House in Macon, Georgia, at their outdoor stage.

AUGUST 27, 1970

MIAMI BEACH CONVENTION CENTER

MIAMI BEACH, FLORIDA

Much has been written about when Duane Allman first met Eric Clapton. There has been some confusion as to whether it was August 26, 1970, or August 27, 1970. Copies of internal management correspondence documents and a telegram to me published on the well-researched online Duane Allman Chronology indicate it to be the latter date. In any event, the concert was held outdoors at the convention center, and I believe was free to the public. The Allman Brothers Band received a fee from the City of Miami Beach.

Eric Clapton, Bobby Whitlock, Carl Radle, and Jim Gordon, along with producer Tom Dowd, had just arrived in town to begin to record what would become the Layla album by Derek and the Dominos. Duane had called Tom Dowd wanting to meet Eric, and when advised, Eric decided to come to the concert with his band members and Tom Dowd. A photographer's pit was located between the stage and a wooden barrier unseen by the audience. Well into the concert, The Allman Brothers Band was shocked to look down and see the group filing in and sitting down to watch and listen. I was shocked as well because I had been unaware they were coming.

Afterwards, we all went over to Criteria Studios, where Eric was awed by a playback of Duane's slide guitar on the soon-to-be-released song "Don't Keep Me Wonderin'" from the in-progress *Idlewild South* album. I can still see the expression on Eric's face in my mind's eye. There followed much conversation, socializing, and jamming in the studio. There was little doubt Duane would be invited to play on the Layla sessions, and although everyone was thrilled, it would ultimately almost break up the band.

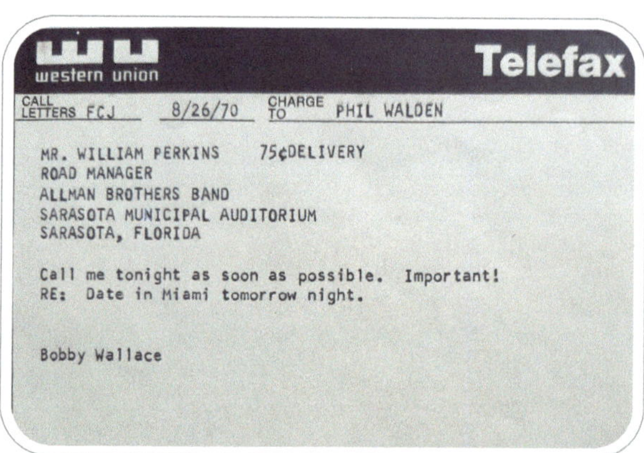

western union Telefax

CALL LETTERS FCJ 8/26/70 CHARGE TO PHIL WALDEN

MR. WILLIAM PERKINS 75¢DELIVERY
ROAD MANAGER
ALLMAN BROTHERS BAND
SARASOTA MUNICIPAL AUDITORIUM
SARASOTA, FLORIDA

Call me tonight as soon as possible. Important!
RE: Date in Miami tomorrow night.

Bobby Wallace

SEPTEMBER 8–9, 1970

RUSH UP

CHICAGO

The Rush Up was a small rock club located at 907 North Rush Street in Chicago. It featured local and up-and-coming national bands and was a popular hangout for famous musicians passing through Chicago. The Allman Brothers Band received only $1,500 for the two nights there. I remember little about this gig other than Duane being absent as he finished the Layla sessions in Miami and the club being a terrible load-in up a steep staircase. Also, I recall shooting pool with Gregg. Neither of us was very good, but I did manage to beat him that time.

Upon returning to Macon, we all had a meeting in manager Phil Walden's office to discuss Duane's absences. He would play two concerts with Eric Clapton in Tampa and Syracuse and be offered a permanent position in Eric's band. After much soul-searching, he declined. Duane promised us all he would make The Allman Brothers Band his number-one priority and keep outside projects to a minimum. Thankfully, he kept that promise. Otherwise, dozens of concerts and the seminal "Live at Filmore East" would have been missed.

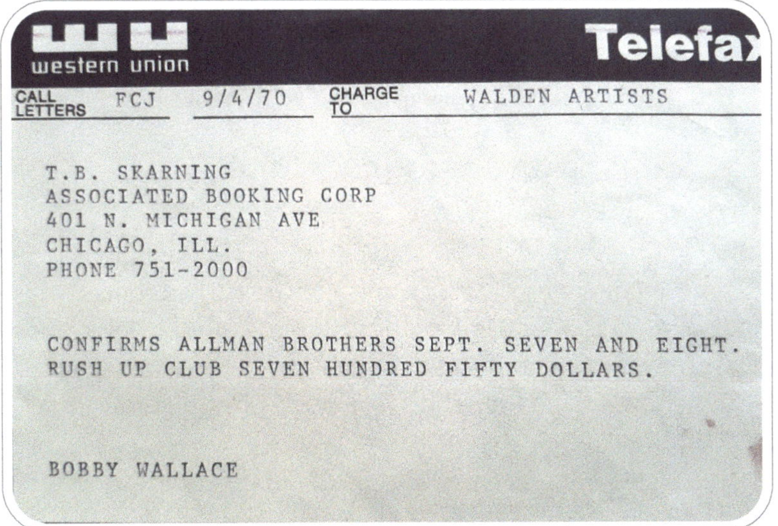

western union Telefax

CALL LETTERS FCJ 9/4/70 CHARGE TO WALDEN ARTISTS

T.B. SKARNING
ASSOCIATED BOOKING CORP
401 N. MICHIGAN AVE
CHICAGO, ILL.
PHONE 751-2000

CONFIRMS ALLMAN BROTHERS SEPT. SEVEN AND EIGHT.
RUSH UP CLUB SEVEN HUNDRED FIFTY DOLLARS.

BOBBY WALLACE

SEPTEMBER 13, 1970

CONTINENTAL CLUB

HOUSTON

We had successfully completed concerts in San Antonio and Austin and were closing out our short Texas run in Houston with a Sunday show at the Continental Club. Club owner Don Robey was a sort of folk hero to us because he also owned Duke Records, home of Bobby "Blue" Bland and some other of our favorite artists. He was also well known for sometimes engaging in questionable business practices.

Upon arriving at the venue, we found no crew, no Mr. Robey, and we were told the show had been cancelled with no explanation and no contact information for Mr. Robey beyond the club. We were all very disappointed, and there were fans outside lining up to enter the building. It was a stark reminder that your heroes may, as the biblical term says, have "feet of clay." I contacted a local rock radio station and underground newspaper, and Berry Oakley with other band members did an interview explaining why we didn't appear. Excerpts from that interview run in a loop in the Oakley family quarters at the Big House Museum in Macon.

SEPTEMBER 16, 1970

PEABODY AUDITORIUM

DAYTONA BEACH, FLORIDA

Headlining the 2,500-seat Peabody Auditorium in Daytona Beach represented a homecoming of sorts for Duane and Gregg. The concert was sponsored and promoted by the Daytona Beach Junior College. Ticket prices were two dollars for students and three dollars for the general public. What a deal! At this show Duane traded his "goldtop" Gibson guitar for a "cherry sunburst" Gibson.

CONTRACT BLANK

AMERICAN FEDERATION OF MUSICIANS OF THE UNITED STATES AND CANADA
(HEREIN CALLED "FEDERATION")

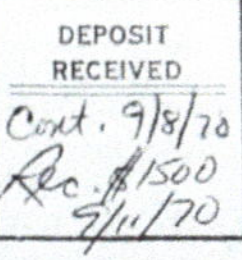

Artists and Promotions
Macon, Georgia 31208
(912) 745 - 8511
P. O. BOX 5127

AFM#373

LOCAL NUMBER 359

THIS CONTRACT for the personal services of musicians on the engagement described below, made this 31st day of August 1970 between the undersigned Purchaser of Music (herein called "Employer") and six(6) (including leader) musicians.*

The musicians are engaged severally on the terms and conditions on the face hereof. The leader represents that the musicians already designated have agreed to be bound by said terms and conditions. Each musician yet to be chosen, upon acceptance, shall be bound by said terms and conditions. Each musician may enforce this agreement. The musicians severally agree to render services under the undersigned leader.

1. Name and Address of Place of Engagement PEABODY AUDITORIUM DAYTONA BEACH, FLORIDA
2. Date(s), starting and finishing time of engagement September 16, 1970 Artists agree to perform one(1) show between 9pm and 11pm.
3. Type of Engagement (specify whether dance, stage show, banquet, etc.) CONCERT FEATURING: ALLMAN BROTHERS BAND
4. WAGE AGREED UPON $ THREE THOUSAND AND NO/100--------------($3000.00)------------ (Terms and Amount)

This wage includes expenses agreed to be reimbursed by the Employer in accordance with the attached schedule, or a schedule to be furnished the Employer on or before the date of engagement.

5. Employer will make payments as follows: SEE ATTACHED RIDER (Specify when payments are to be made)

Upon request by the Federation or the local in whose jurisdiction the musicians shall perform hereunder, Employer either shall make advance payment hereunder or shall post an appropriate bond.

If the engagement is subject to contribution to the A.F.M. & E.P.W. Pension Welfare Fund, the leader will collect same from the Employer and pay it to the Fund; and the Employer and leader agree to be bound by the Trust Indenture dated October 2, 1959, as amended, relating to services rendered hereunder in the U. S., and by the Agreement and Declaration of Trust dated April 9, 1962, as amended, relating to services rendered hereunder in Canada.

6. The Employer is hereby given an option to extend this agreement for a period of XXXXXXXXX weeks beyond the original term thereof. Said option can be exercised only by written notice from the Employer to the musicians, not later than XXXXXX days prior to the expiration of the original term, and a copy of said notice shall be filed with the Federation local in whose jurisdiction the engagement is to be played.

7. The Employer shall at all times have complete supervision, direction and control over the services of musicians on this engagement and expressly reserves the right to control the manner, means and details of the performance of services by the musicians including the leader as well as the ends to be accomplished. If any musicians have not been chosen upon the signing of this contract, the leader shall, as agent for the Employer and under his instructions, hire such persons and any replacements as are required.

8. In accordance with the Constitution, By-laws Rules and Regulations of the Federation, the parties will submit every claim, dispute, controversy or difference involving the musical services arising out of or connected with this contract and the engagement covered thereby for determination by the International Executive Board of the Federation or a similar board of an appropriate local thereof and such determination shall be conclusive, final and binding upon the parties.

TO BE MONEY ORDER **ADDITIONAL TERMS AND CONDITIONS** ~~CERTIFIED OR CASHIERS CHECK~~

The leader shall, as agent of the Employer, enforce disciplinary measures for just cause, and carry out instructions as to selections and manner of performance. The agreement of the musicians to perform is subject to proven detention by sickness, accidents, riots, strikes, epidemics, acts of God, or any other legitimate conditions beyond their control. On behalf of the Employer the leader will distribute the amount received from the Employer to the musicians, including himself as indicated on the opposite side of this contract, or in place thereof on separate memorandum supplied to the Employer at or before the commencement of the employment hereunder and take and turn over to the Employer receipts therefor from each musician, including himself. The amount paid to the leader includes the cost of transportation, which will be reported by the leader to the Employer.

All employees covered by this agreement must be members in good standing of the Federation. However, if the employment provided for hereunder is subject to the Labor-Management Relations Act, 1947, all employees who are members of the Federation when their employment commences hereunder shall be continued in such employment only so long as they continue such membership in good standing. All other employees covered by this agreement, on or before the thirtieth day following the commencement of their employment, or the effective date of this agreement, whichever is later, shall become and continue to be members in good standing of the Federation. The provisions of this paragraph shall not become effective unless and until permitted by applicable law.

To the extent permitted by applicable law, nothing in this contract shall ever be construed so as to interfere with any duty owing by any musician performing hereunder to the Federation pursuant to its Constitution, By-laws, Rules, Regulations and Orders.

Any musicians on this engagement are free to cease service hereunder by reason of any strike, ban, unfair list order or requirement of the Federation, and shall be free to accept and engage in other employment of the same or similar character or otherwise, without any restraint, hindrance, penalty, obligation or liability whatever, any other provisions of this contract to the contrary notwithstanding.

Representatives of the Federation local in whose jurisdiction the musicians shall perform hereunder shall have access to the place of performance (except to private residences) for the purpose of conferring with the musicians.

No performance on the engagement shall be recorded, reproduced or transmitted from the place of performance, in any manner or by any means whatsoever, in the absence of a specific written agreement with the Federation relating to and permitting such recording, reproduction or transmission.

The Employer represents that there does not exist against him, in favor of any member of the Federation, any claim of any kind arising out of musical services rendered for such Employer. No musician will be required to perform any provisions of this contract or to render any services for said Employer as long as any such claim is unsatisfied or unpaid, in whole or in part. If the Employer breaches this agreement, he shall pay the musicians in addition to damages, 6% interest thereon plus a reasonable attorney's fee.

To the extent permitted by applicable law, all of the Constitution, By-laws, Rules and Regulations of the Federation and of any local thereof applicable to this engagement (not in conflict with those of the Federation) will be adhered to and the parties acknowledge that they are and each has the obligation to be, fully acquainted therewith.

Mr. Bob Boyd, Mr. Dan Stout Print Employer's Name	DUANE ALLMAN 601 Print Leader's Name Local No.
X F. E. O'Connell, Robert Boyd Signature of Employer	X Duane Allman Signature of Leader
Student Government Assoc. Print Street Address	C/O 535 Cotton Avenue Print Street Address
Daytona Beach Jr. College, Daytona Beach, City State	Macon Georgia City State
Florida	WALDEN ARTISTS

SEPTEMBER 20, 1970

RFK STADIUM

WASHINGTON, DC

The Berlin Airlift Concert was held outdoors at the Robert F. Kennedy Stadium in Washington, DC. It headlined Grand Funk Railroad with The Allman Brothers Band, Pacific Gas and Electric, and other supporting bands. I believe this was the very first concert where the band received a $4,000 guarantee. I remember manager Phil Walden having dinner at my apartment soon thereafter where we discussed the next guarantee plateaus of $5,000 and then $7,500. Those goals were soon met and surpassed.

SEPTEMBER 23, 1970

FILLMORE EAST

NEW YORK, NEW YORK

Performers for this taping of NET's (now PBS) television show "Welcome to Filmore East" included The Allman Brothers Band, Elvin Bishop, the Byrds, Albert King, Van Morrison, and Sha-Na-Na. Video exists of the band, introduced by Bill Graham, performing "Don't Keep Me Wonderin'," "Dreams," "In Memory of Elizabeth Reed," and "Whipping Post."

N.E.T.
presents
"WELCOME
TO
FILLMORE EAST"
with
(in alphabetical order)
ALLMAN BROTHERS
ELVIN BISHOP GROUP
BYRDS
FLOCK
ALBERT KING
VAN MORRISON
SHA-NA-NA
JOE'S LIGHTS
HOST: BILL GRAHAM
FILLMORE EAST
September 23, 1970
C 107
Good Only
WED. 7:00 P.M.
SEPT'BER
23
1970
FILLMORE EAST
$1.50
1st BALCONY
SEPT. 23, 1970
1.50
REFUND

OCTOBER 9, 1970

FLORIDA STATE UNIVERSITY

TALLAHASSEE, FLORIDA

The band performed a homecoming concert in Tully Gym at Florida State University in Tallahassee with Frank Zappa. Because of homecoming, all hotels and motels for miles around were filled, so we were housed in a school recreation facility at a nearby lake. The band enjoyed some fishing and boating. Noted photographer Stephen Paley had taken some photos of the band the night before at Berry College in Rome, Georgia, and took more at the lake in Tallahassee. Some of the Tallahassee photos were used on the first Duane Allman anthology album.

I remember when a school official took me inside an office in the gym to get paid, there sat Frank Zappa in an office chair behind a desk deep in sleep and snoring loudly. I can still see that image as if it were yesterday.

OCTOBER 10, 1970

JAI-ALAI FRONTON

MIAMI

The next gig required an overnight drive (or "jump") from Tallahassee to Miami for a concert at the Miami Jai-Alai (pronounced hi-li) Fronton. Jai alai is a sporting-event contest that originated in Spain and is popular in Latin America and Florida. It features pari-mutuel betting on the outcomes and remains existent today. The privately owned building seated up to 6,500 and hosted hundreds of rock concerts over the years. Many were promoted by Leas Campbell, a young hippie turned businessman/

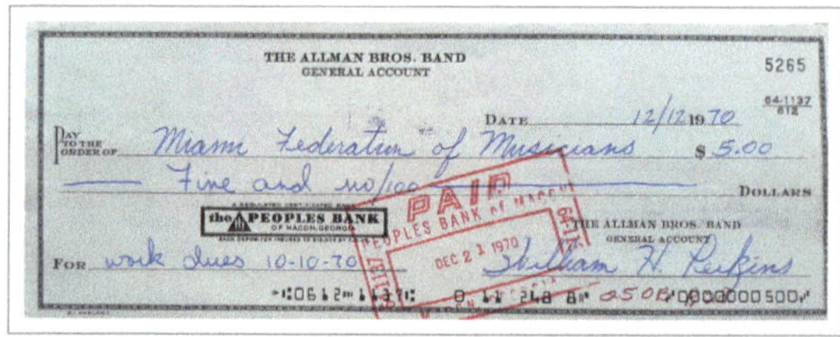

THE ALLMAN BROS. BAND
GENERAL ACCOUNT
5265
64-1137 / 612
DATE 12/12 1970
PAY TO THE ORDER OF Miami Federation of Musicians $ 5.00
Five and no/100 DOLLARS
the PEOPLES BANK OF MACON, GEORGIA
PAID PEOPLES BANK of MACON DEC 2 1 1970
THE ALLMAN BROS. BAND
GENERAL ACCOUNT
FOR work dues 10-10-70
William H. Perkins

concert promoter. He became a good friend and supporter of The Allman Brothers Band. It is rumored that his first financing came from an enterprising group of marijuana smugglers.

OCTOBER 17, 1970

THE SITAR

SPARTANBURG, SOUTH CAROLINA

The Allman Brothers Band was becoming very popular in the Carolinas, and Spartanburg was a smaller market in the northwestern section of South Carolina. The band was guaranteed a $3,000 fee, which was top money for a market of that size at that time.

Toy Factory, the band that opened the concert, was named after their leader and founder, Toy Caldwell; they later became the Marshall Tucker Band (named after a local blind piano tuner).

OCTOBER 23, 1970

SUNY STONY BROOK

STONY BROOK, NEW YORK

And yet again we played the State University of New York at Stony Brook. This time the band was co-headlined with Delaney, Bonnie & Friends, who closed the show. Duane was great friends with them, and he, too, would sometimes sit in with them as a "friend."

Delaney Bramlett and his wife, Bonnie Bramlett, had an ever-changing group of "friends" who performed and recorded with them during their most active years of 1969 through 1972. The "friends" included Bobby Whitlock, Dave Mason, King Curtis, Rita Coolidge, Eric Clapton, and Duane Allman, among others.

OCTOBER 30, 1970

VANDERBILT UNIVERSITY

NASHVILLE, TENNESSEE

This began as another routine college concert performance, with the band opening for Jesse Colin Young and the Youngbloods. After the show back at the hotel, I recall that the band members had obtained a small chunk of opium. Later, I was alerted that Duane had experimented with the opium and become comatose. We rushed him to the nearby Vanderbilt University Hospital, where he was admitted in grave condition with no guarantee of recovery. I remember calling Bunky Odom of the Walden office back in Macon and notifying him of the situation. All of the band and crew huddled in worry, and Berry Oakley prayed for at least one more year together. After several hours of fearing the worst, we were advised that Duane had stabilized and was out of danger. He would be held for observation in the hospital for twenty-four hours before becoming eligible for release. In much better spirits, we headed for Atlanta without Duane for a concert the following evening.

HAMMOND ORGAN STUDIOS
OF NASHVILLE, INC.
100 Oaks Shopping Center
NASHVILLE, TENNESSEE 37204
615 291-2233

№ 1460

SERVICE / INSTALL / PICK UP / DELIVER / PHONE / REPAIR IN HOME / SHOP / DATE OF ORDER 10/30/70

NAME GREGG ALLMAN
ADDRESS HOLLIDAY INN
CITY NASHVILLE TENN
MAKE HAMMOND MODEL LESLIE B3 122 SERIAL NO. / C.O.D. / CHARGE

NATURE OF SERVICE REQUEST / DATE PROMISED

QUAN	PART NO.	DESCRIPTION	PRICE	AMOUNT
1		adapter solut.		1 85
1		neoprene tire		75

Paid in Full
Cash 10/30/70
D.McC.

SERVICE PERFORMED: Repair Leslie motor assembly

TOTAL MATERIAL	2 60
TECHNICAL SERVICE TIME	10 00
TAX	54
TOTAL	12 54

Thank You! DATE COMPLETED / / CASH ON COMPLETION OF WORK →

INVOICE COPY

I hereby accept above performed service, and charges, as being satisfactory and acknowledge that equipment has been left in good condition

Technician ______ Customer's Signature ______

GUARANTEE: We are pleased to guarantee all parts installed by us against normal service failure for a period of 90 days. See detailed guarantee on reverse side.

OCTOBER 31, 1970

EMORY UNIVERSITY

ATLANTA

Duane Allman was in good condition but not yet discharged from the hospital in Nashville. We would have to play a rare date without him at Emory University in Atlanta. The school administration was very disappointed that he would not appear, and they asked for a reduction in our fee, which we granted. The concert was well received by the students and fans. Even without Duane, the five-member Allman Brothers Band could still play circles around their peers.

NOVEMBER 1, 1970

PARK CENTER

CHARLOTTE, NORTH CAROLINA

Another familiar venue was the three thousand-seat Park Center in Charlotte, North Carolina, promoted by Cecil Corbett. His company, Beach Club Promotions, was named after his popular Myrtle Beach, South Carolina, nightclub. Cecil was an early supporter of the band and one of my favorite promoters. A fully recovered Duane Allman arrived separately on a commercial airline flight from Nashville. He sincerely promised us he would never repeat the conduct that occurred in Nashville, and he never did. That is not to say his experimentation with drugs would not continue. There was, however, a certain amount of caution and moderation.

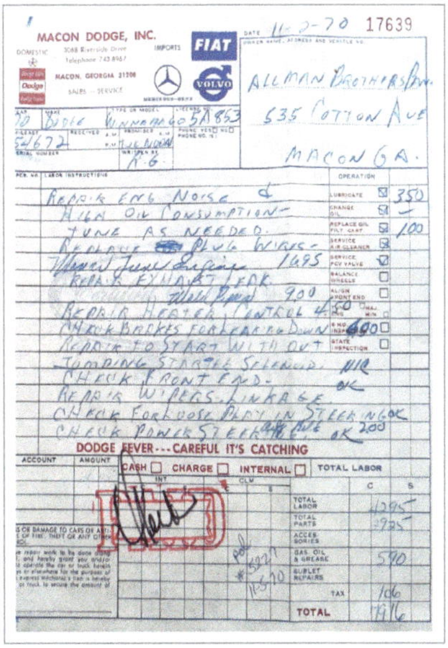
MACON DODGE, INC.
3088 Riverside Drive
Telephone 743-8967
MACON, GEORGIA 31206
SALES — SERVICE
DOMESTIC IMPORTS
FIAT
MERCEDES-BENZ
VOLVO

DATE 11-2-70 17639

ALLMAN BROTHERS BAND
535 COTTON AVE
MACON GA.

YEAR 70 MAKE DODGE TYPE OR MODEL WINNEBAGO LICENSE NO. 5A853
MILEAGE 54672 PROMISED TUE NOON
WRITTEN BY R.G.

LABOR INSTRUCTIONS

REPAIR ENG NOISE &
HIGH OIL CONSUMPTION—
TUNE AS NEEDED.
REPLACE PLUG WIRES— 1695
REPAIR EXHAUST LEAK.
900
REPAIR HEATER CONTROL 450
CHECK BRAKES FOR LEAKING DOWN 600
REPAIR TO START WITHOUT
JUMPING STARTER SOLENOID. N/R
CHECK FRONT END. OK
REPAIR WIPERS LINKAGE.
CHECK FOR LOOSE PLAY IN STEERING OK
CHECK POWER STEERING. OK 200

OPERATION	
LUBRICATE	350
CHANGE OIL	—
REPLACE OIL FILT. CART	100
SERVICE AIR CLEANER	
SERVICE PCV VALVE	
BALANCE WHEELS	
ALIGN FRONT END	
ENG. TUNE MAJ. MIN.	
STATE INSPECTION	

DODGE FEVER---CAREFUL IT'S CATCHING

ACCOUNT AMOUNT CASH CHARGE INTERNAL TOTAL LABOR

TOTAL LABOR	4295
TOTAL PARTS	2925
ACCESSORIES	
GAS, OIL & GREASE	590
SUBLET REPAIRS	
TAX	106
TOTAL	7916

NOVEMBER 6, 1970

TULANE UNIVERSITY

NEW ORLEANS

Most college concerts were attended by contemporary, semi-hippie-styled students. At Tulane University in New Orleans we found ourselves before a very conservative coat-and-tie- and party-dress-wearing group of "Freddy Frat" and "Susie Sorority" types, and the band was somewhat befuddled. After many audience requests for some hit parade classics, the band complied with tongues firmly planted in cheek. I even chimed in on background vocals from the side of the stage. This was an unusual situation, and I don't think the audience ever caught on to the joke.

NOVEMBER 7, 1970

THE WAREHOUSE

NEW ORLEANS

We stayed over in New Orleans for a concert the following evening in the much friendlier and more familiar confines of the Warehouse. The Allman Brothers Band was in the middle slot, with Les Moore opening and Procol Harum headlining. The ticket price was four dollars. Once again, as so often happened, The Allman Brothers Band stole the show. Procol Harum's sound engineer referred to his employers as "Procol Ho-Hum." He soon jumped ship, and we hired his company to provide the sound system for our shows whenever possible.

DELTA AIR LINES, INC.

If the passenger's journey involves an ultimate destination or stop in a country other than the country of departure, the Warsaw Convention may be applicable and the Convention governs and in most cases limits the liability of carriers for death or personal injury and in respect of loss of or damage to baggage.

PASSENGER TICKET AND BAGGAGE CHECK
PASSENGER'S COUPON

006 43249072

DELTA AIR LINES, INC.
NOV =8'70
FTO-13
NEW ORLEANS, LA.

NAME OF PASSENGER: DICK BETTS
NOT TRANSFERABLE

NOT GOOD FOR PASSAGE

	CARRIER	FLIGHT/CLASS	DATE	TIME	STATUS
FROM VOID					
TO VOID					
TO NEW ORLEANS	DL	0106F	08NOV	012 0P	OK
TO ATLANTA	DL	0110F	08NOV	042 0P	OK
TO CHARLOTTE					

FARE X — TOTAL $ 65.00

AIRLINE CODE 006 — FORM AND SERIAL NUMBER 432490727 4

Issued By — SOLD SUBJECT TO CONDITIONS OF CONTRACT ON PASSENGER'S COUPON

DELTA AIR LINES, INC.

If the passenger's journey involves an ultimate destination or stop in a country other than the country of departure, the Warsaw Convention may be applicable and the Convention governs and in most cases limits the liability of carriers for death or personal injury and in respect of loss of or damage to baggage.

PASSENGER TICKET AND BAGGAGE CHECK
PASSENGER'S COUPON

006 43249074

AIR LINES, INC.
NOV =8'70
FTO-13
NEW ORLEANS, LA.

NAME OF PASSENGER: D ALLMAN
NOT TRANSFERABLE

NOT GOOD FOR PASSAGE

	CARRIER	FLIGHT/CLASS	DATE	TIME	STATUS
FROM VOID					
TO VOID					
TO VOID					
TO NEW ORLEANS	DL	0106F	08NOV	012 0P	OK
TO ATLANTA					

FARE X — TOTAL $ 48.00

AIRLINE CODE 006 — FORM AND SERIAL NUMBER 432490742 5

Issued By — SOLD SUBJECT TO CONDITIONS OF CONTRACT ON PASSENGER'S COUPON

DELTA AIR LINES, INC.

If the passenger's journey involves an ultimate destination or stop in a country other than the country of departure, the Warsaw Convention may be applicable and the Convention governs and in most cases limits the liability of carriers for death or personal injury and in respect of loss of or damage to baggage.

PASSENGER TICKET AND BAGGAGE CHECK
PASSENGER'S COUPON

006 43249074

AIR LINES, INC.
NOV =8'70
FTO-13
NEW ORLEANS, LA.

NAME OF PASSENGER: G ALLMAN
NOT TRANSFERABLE

NOT GOOD FOR PASSAGE

	CARRIER	FLIGHT/CLASS	DATE	TIME	STATUS
FROM VOID					
TO VOID					
TO VOID					
TO NEW ORLEANS	DL	0106F	08NOV	012 0P	OK
TO ATLANTA					

FARE X — TOTAL $ 48.00

AIRLINE CODE 006 — FORM AND SERIAL NUMBER 432490743 6

NOVEMBER 19–21, 1970

BOSTON TEA PARTY

BOSTON

The Allman Brothers Band headlined the Boston Tea Party with opener Brethren. They had played some of their very first shows there in the summer of 1969 before their first album was released in the fall. Then they had crashed rent free for some time in a vacant apartment that Twiggs provided with electricity to power the equipment with by running an extension cord to an adjacent apartment. We had hotel rooms this time. The Boston Tea Party was one of the last remaining "ballroom" venues on the East Coast. Others included the Electric Factory in Philadelphia and Ludlow's Garage in Cincinnati. The Tea Party was owned by promoter Don Law, a good friend of band manager Phil Walden. Don was an early and ardent supporter of the band and would go on to promote many shows throughout New England over the years.

September 15, 1970

Mr. Don Law
Boston Tea Party
15 Lansdown Street
Boston, Massachusetts

Dear Don:

Enclosed are two (2) advance copies on IDLEWILD SOUTH by THE ALLMAN BROTHERS BAND. Please pass them on to WBCN.

I asked Jon Podell to get together with you on a November date with the ALLMAN BROTHERS BAND.

Many thanks!

Warmest regards.

Sincerely,

Phil Walden

DECEMBER 11, 1970

FILLMORE EAST

NEW YORK, NEW YORK

Top ticket price at Fillmore East was $5.50 for orchestra seats as Canned Heat headlined and closed the show, preceded by The Allman Brothers Band along with supporting bands Dreams and Toe Fat. Joe's Lights provided the spectacular lighting effects. Canned Heat with Bob "The Bear" Hite was a favorite of mine, but The Allman Brothers Band once again seemed to be the crowd favorite. They continued to grow in audience appeal and ticket-selling ability in New York and the entire northeastern area of the country. Major headline events would soon follow in the upcoming new year.

DECEMBER 18, 1970

THE FORUM

LOS ANGELES

The Allman Brothers Band opened for Three Dog Night at the 17,500-seat Forum in Los Angeles. This was a "career" date, which occurs when a less well-known, or "baby band," opens for an established national act for low money at a large venue in a major metropolitan market. Los Angeles was second only to New York City in that respect. It takes a smart and influential personal manager along with a certain amount of "buzz" from the band to obtain one of these coveted spots. It is done with the hope of gaining visibility with the national press and influential industry figures. The band has to deliver the goods, and The Allman Brothers Band always did.

This was my first trip to Los Angeles. The fact that I was a huge movie buff made it all the more exciting for me. We stayed at the Tropicana Motel on Santa Monica Boulevard. Hall of Fame baseball pitcher Sandy Koufax originally owned the motel, and it was a haven for rock bands in the 1970s. Tom

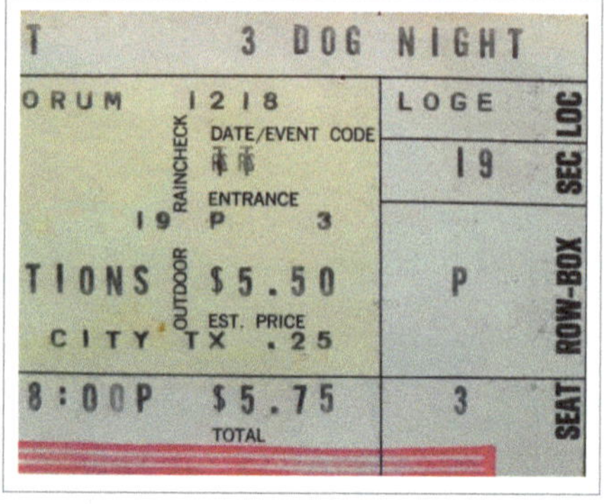

Waits lived there, and frequent guests included Jim Morrison, Janis Joplin, Bob Marley, Alice Cooper, Iggy Pop, Blondie, the Ramones, and many others, including many Los Angeles-based bands and solo artists. An era ended when it was torn down in 1987.

Atlantic Records, distributors of the band's label, Capricorn Records, provided us with limousine service for our very first time. Little did I know then that I would be renting fleets of limos in the near future.

SHIP AND SHORE TRAVEL AGENCY
679 WALNUT ST.
MACON, GEORGIA 31201
912-743-9553

INVOICE
No. 143
DATE December 230
REF.
TOUR
FIT
LEAVING

Name Willaim Perkins Group c/o Redwall
Address 535 Cherry Street
Macon, Georgia Zip

A/C William Perkins:
For: Mr. William Perkins
Mr. Gregg Allman
Mr. Duane Allman
Mr. Dickie Betts
Mr. Barry Oakley
Mr. Johny Johnson
Mr. Butch Trucks
Mr. Larry Campbell
Mr. Kim Payne

9 Economy at $84.00	756	00
½ fare cabin baggage	42	00

ATEO # 006-99-057-245/6
3 doubles and one triple, De Ville Motel 2200 Tulane New Orleans- in Dec. 30- out January 01 (rooms are good until Jan. 02 if the group would like to remain; These accommodations were available only at the package rate because of the Bowl Game on New Year's Day

$82.68 per room x 4	330	72

DECEMBER 31, 1970

THE WAREHOUSE

NEW ORLEANS

We closed the year with a fantastic show with Dr. John the Night-Tripper at the Warehouse in New Orleans. We celebrated with a great party with friends and family, and spirits were high heading into the new year. We were playing this venue so often that Warehouse historians now consider The Allman Brothers Band as their official "house band." They have released a limited-edition poster memorializing that fact.

I concluded my first six months with The Allman Brothers Band on an upbeat note. The band was just starting to turn the corner financially and really beginning to "happen" nationally. The work was difficult and mentally and physically exhausting, but rewarding. I loved the band, crew, and family, and they all seemed to accept me and appreciate my hard work and dedication. We were truly a brother- and sisterhood. 1971 would bring us all triumph and tragedy.

1971

JANUARY 7, 1971

GEORGIA SOUTHERN UNIVERSITY

STATESBORO, GEORGIA

Our first concert in the new year 1971 was at Georgia Southern University in Statesboro, Georgia, about halfway between Macon and Savannah. Needless to say, the band's version of Blind Willie McTell's blues classic "Statesboro Blues" was a big favorite there and was greeted with thunderous applause.

The band earned a guarantee of $2,500 plus an overage bonus of $525. Basically, after box office receipts cover the band's guaranteed fee, all concert-related expenses, and a 10 to 15 percent profit to the promoter, any remaining receipts are split on a negotiated percentage basis between the band and the promoter, with the band receiving the larger share. In any event, the band would receive no less than their guaranteed fee. These situations occurred much more frequently as the band's popularity increased, and on some occasions the band's percentage overage bonus would be larger than the guarantee, as you will see.

JANUARY 16, 1971

MUNICIPAL AUDITORIUM

ATLANTA

The Allman Brothers Band returned to Atlanta to headline the five thousand-seat Municipal Auditorium for promoter Alex Cooley. The Hampton Grease Band featuring Colonel Bruce Hampton opened the show. Colonel Bruce remained a friend of band members until his recent passing. The band earned a $5,000 guarantee plus an additional $6,213 in performance overage bonus. The show was a huge creative and financial success, and we were beginning to be able to pay off some of the band's large accumulated debt.

The band's rise to stardom in Atlanta did not follow the usual formula for success. Typically, a young band would start in very small clubs and, if popular, build slowly to larger venues, then on to open, and finally headline major concerts. In Atlanta, The Allman Brothers Band began with free, impromptu concerts in Piedmont Park and then, for the most part, skipped performing shows in smaller clubs and jumped straight into opening and, soon thereafter, headlining concerts at the city's then major venue, the Municipal Auditorium. It was another example of how their career success sometimes followed unconventional methods.

JANUARY 17, 1971

SYRIA MOSQUE

PITTSBURGH

We didn't have much time to celebrate the Atlanta show as we had a 724-mile jump to Pittsburgh for a concert the following evening. Ordinarily, we would have left after the Atlanta show and driven the roughly fifteen-hour trip, but the band preferred to stay the night in Atlanta and fly the following day, which we did.

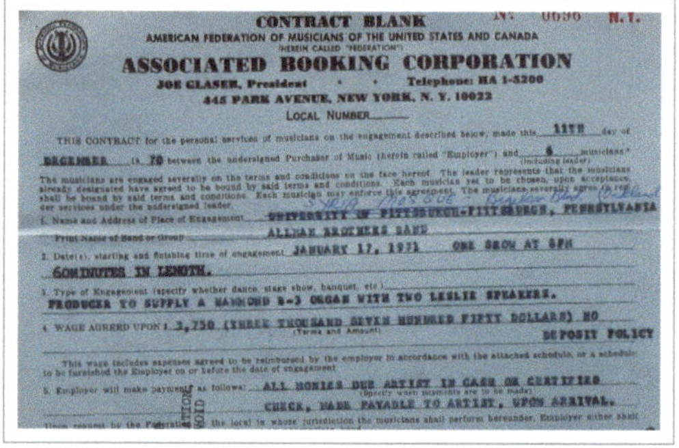

CONTRACT BLANK
AMERICAN FEDERATION OF MUSICIANS OF THE UNITED STATES AND CANADA
(HEREIN CALLED "FEDERATION")
ASSOCIATED BOOKING CORPORATION
JOE GLASER, President • • Telephone: HA 1-5200
445 PARK AVENUE, NEW YORK, N. Y. 10022
LOCAL NUMBER ______

THIS CONTRACT for the personal services of musicians on the engagement described below, made this 11TH day of DECEMBER 19 70 between the undersigned Purchaser of Music (herein called "Employer") and 6 musicians (including leader). The musicians are engaged severally on the terms and conditions on the face hereof. The leader represents that the musicians already designated have agreed to be bound by said terms and conditions. Each musician yet to be chosen, upon acceptance, shall be bound by said terms and conditions. Each musician may enforce this agreement. The musicians severally agree to render services under the undersigned leader.

1. Name and Address of Place of Engagement: UNIVERSITY OF PITTSBURGH-PITTSBURGH, PENNSYLVANIA
Print Name of Band or Group: ALLMAN BROTHERS BAND
2. Date(s), starting and finishing time of engagement: JANUARY 17, 1971 ONE SHOW AT 8PM 60MINUTES IN LENGTH.
3. Type of Engagement (specify whether dance, stage show, banquet, etc.): PRODUCER TO SUPPLY A HAMMOND B-3 ORGAN WITH TWO LESLIE SPEAKERS.
4. WAGE AGREED UPON $ 3,750 (THREE THOUSAND SEVEN HUNDRED FIFTY DOLLARS) NO DEPOSIT POLICY
(Terms and Amount)

This wage includes expenses agreed to be reimbursed by the employer in accordance with the attached schedule, or a schedule to be furnished the Employer on or before the date of engagement.

5. Employer will make payments as follows: ALL MONIES DUE ARTIST IN CASH OR CERTIFIED CHECK, MADE PAYABLE TO ARTIST, UPON ARRIVAL.
(Specify when payments are to be made)

The band was the middle act on a show with Taj Mahal opening and Little Richard closing. Each band received equal-size billing in all print ads and posters, and The Allman Brothers Band received a flat fee of $3,750. It was a great show on a cold night remembered by many.

The Syria Mosque was an ornate Middle Eastern-themed building built for the Shriners in the early 1900s with a capacity of 3,700. It was the scene of concerts by such varied artists as opera star Enrico Caruso, bandleaders

John Philip Souza and Benny Goodman, and dozens of premier rock bands over the years. Despite efforts to preserve it as a historical landmark, it was demolished in 1991. Many other great venues would meet a similar fate.

JANUARY 22–23, 1971

CAPITOL THEATRE

PORT CHESTER, NEW YORK

It was party time again as we were with good friends Delaney and Bonnie & Friends at promoter Howard Stein's Capitol Theatre in Port Chester, New York, just north of New York City. The Allman Brothers Band received a $4,000 flat fee as the middle act with Bert Sommer opening.

The 1,800-seat Capitol was built as a movie theater in 1926. It was hugely popular in the 1970s as a rock venue before eventually closing because of problems with a local evening-noise ordinance. It was reopened as a concert venue again in 2011 and still operates today. Howard Stein was the primary promoter there and would also produce Allman Brothers Band concerts in Atlanta, Miami, and New York City. He eventually tired of dealing with rock bands and became a successful owner of several trendy New York City discos and nightclubs. He passed away from cancer at age sixty-two in 2007.

JANUARY 28–31, 1971

SAN FRANCISCO

West Coast trips were inherently expensive due to travel costs alone. Combine that with low concert fees and you have a guaranteed financial loss. It was necessary for visibility and viability reasons and career building to play the West Coast as much as possible and "bite the bullet" on the financial loss—we could and would make up the losses elsewhere. Other than the Los Angeles, San Francisco, and San Diego markets, The Allman Brothers Band was never as big in the far West as they were in the South and East.

The band was middle billed on a show headlined by Hot Tuna and opened by the twenty-four piece Trinidad Tripoli Steel Band at Bill Graham's Fillmore West. The band earned a flat fee of just $3,000 for the four days. It was a great show with a colorful advertising poster. Originals of that poster bring a huge price today, but beware of reprints.

Some sources claim one show of the run was moved to Winterland arena for unspecified scheduling reasons, but I have no memory or records to confirm that. Noted band historian, tour manager, and discologist Kirk West agrees with my recollections.

FEBRUARY 1–3, 1971

WHISKY A GO GO

LOS ANGELES

We headed down the coast to appear next at the five hundred-seat Whisky a Go Go in Los Angeles for a $1,500 flat fee for the entire three-day run. Again, this was a career-building promotional date and not a moneymaker.

The Whisky, as it was called, was opened in 1964 by former Chicago cop Elmer Valentine. He was cofounder of the Whisky, the Roxy, and the Rainbow Bar & Grill, all trendy Hollywood nightspots. From its inception, the Whisky was a combination disco and concert hall, and white-booted go-go girls apparently originated there. Almost every noted West Coast band and many national and English acts played there. The Doors were the unofficial "house band" because they made so many appearances there. Duane and Gregg Allman were well known at the Whisky, too, thanks to their prior membership in the Los Angeles-based band Hour Glass. In 2006, the Rock and Roll Hall of Fame honored the venue with a marker designating it as a historic rock and roll landmark.

FEBRUARY 4, 1971

OHIO WESLEYAN UNIVERSITY

DELAWARE, OHIO

Occasionally, for various reasons, we had to make nightmarish overnight jumps. This was one of those. Early in the morning after the final Whisky show and late-night partying, I herded the band, crew, and equipment onto an approximately 2,000-mile flight to Columbus, Ohio, followed by an additional drive in rental cars and a truck to the small town of Delaware, Ohio. We were already three hours behind East Coast time when we started, so there was no room for error. We arrived exhausted but with time to spare for an evening concert at Ohio Wesleyan University for a hard-earned $3,500 flat fee. The difficult we did immediately. The impossible took longer.

FEBRUARY 5, 1971

THE SPECTRUM

PHILADELPHIA

Early in 1970, before I joined the band, they purchased, with installment credit cosigned by manager Phil Walden, a Winnebago camper for tour travel. It was a Twiggs Lyndon idea, and a good one at the time. "The Winnie," as we called it, was a comfortable and convenient way to travel. However, it was not designed for continuous heavy-duty operation and soon developed repeated mechanical failures, especially with the automatic transmission. Fortunately, we never missed a show because of these breakdowns. We began flying more and more and would soon retire the Winnebago completely. Thus began the merry-go-round of airport, rental car, hotel, gig then reverse and repeat. It would grind us all down, but nobody complained. The band was thriving on their music.

The morning after the Ohio show, we flew to Philadelphia for a big concert at the Spectrum. By now, our equipment truck and driver had caught up with us. The Chambers Brothers headlined the Spectrum show, and they were preceded by The Allman Brothers Band. Cowboy was the opener with Little Richard to follow and then an intermission. Little Richard was not happy with the sequencing and refused to play in his allotted spot. After a long delay, The Allman Brothers Band began their set only to be interrupted twice by a complaining Little Richard. We were all amused by the first interruption but not the second. Finally, Richard was escorted away by security, and the band completed a blistering and well-reviewed set by the media. The concert drew about thirteen thousand attendees with ticket prices of $4.00 and $4.50. The Allman Brothers Band received a flat fee of $3,500. Never a dull moment.

FEBRUARY 20, 1971

UNIVERSITY OF VERMONT & FRANKLIN PEARCE COLLEGE

BURLINGTON, VERMONT & RINDGE, NEW HAMPSHIRE

Although it was not particularly rare for The Allman Brothers Band to perform two shows in one day, it was virtually unheard of to perform two shows in one day in different cities. In fact, this is the only time I can recall this happening with The Allman Brothers Band. I would do it again with Gregg Allman's solo band in Cleveland and Nashville in the 1980s, but that's a story for another time. The matinee was a rescheduled concert from February 18, and the band opened for the Chambers Brothers at the University of Vermont for a 1:00 P.M. show. After the set, everyone joined in for a super-fast loadout, and roadies Mike Callahan and Kim Payne took off in the equipment truck for an approximate four-hour drive over treacherous, icy, snowy, two-lane backwoods roads. I was really concerned about them getting through on time.

The rest of us took a small commuter-type prop plane to a community airport near remote Rindge, New Hampshire. Students from Franklin Pearce College picked us up and drove us to the campus. I was surprised that Mike and Kim had already arrived and were enjoying snowmobile rides. The evening performance went off without a hitch, and the band received $3,500 flat fees for each show. It was another example of everyone performing error-free logistics and great musicianship when there was no room for error.

MARCH 11–13, 1971

FILLMORE EAST

NEW YORK, NEW YORK

The Allman Brothers Band's first and second albums were released in November 1969 and September 1970, respectively. Each received a generally good response from critics and the record-buying public, but neither met sales expectations. It was difficult to capture the band's power in a grouping of short songs totaling about thirty minutes in length. Later, they would be repackaged as a double album and receive strong sales and a gold record award.

Talks had been underway among the band, their management, and distributor Atlantic Records about a third album. After much discussion, it was agreed that a specially priced two-disc live album of the band in concert would be the best presentation. Recording would take place at a weekend engagement at Bill Graham's Fillmore East in New York City. The Allman Brothers Band was billed as an "extra added attraction" with Johnny Winter and the Elvin Bishop Group. When the first two shows sold out in advance, a third show was added for the preceding Thursday night. The band received a flat $6,250 fee for the three shows.

Everyone felt the resulting recordings finally captured the true essence of the band. The album was released on July 6, 1971, and quickly became a smash hit. *At Filmore East* remains one of the most acclaimed rock albums of all time, and its reception and success became the major breakthrough we had all been seeking. Things began to move even more quickly.

March 17, 1971

Management and Employees
FILLMORE EAST
105 Second Avenue
New York, New York 10003

Dear Friends:

On behalf of myself, the band, and everyone connected with THE ALLMAN BROTHERS BAND organization, I would like to offer our sincere thanks for your cooperation and assistance during the recording of our performance there this past weekend.

As always, you handled everything in an efficient, professional manner, and it certainly makes our job go a lot smoother. It is a genuine pleasure to work with people like you.

Again, thank you. We look forward to working with you again in the near future.

Yours very truly,

Willie Perkins
Road Manager
ALLMAN BROTHERS BAND

WP:rlw

cc: Mr. Bill Graham
Fillmore East Corp.
105 Second Avenue
New York, New York

MARCH 21, 1971

SOUTHWEST LOUISIANA UNIVERSITY

LAFAYETTE, LOUISIANA

Feeling elated from the promising Fillmore East live recordings, we played one more show in Selden, New York, before taking six days off in Macon. We then headed out on a routine series of Southern dates before we were to head north again. After a $4,000 concert at the Warehouse in New Orleans, we traveled in rental cars to Southwest Louisiana University in Lafayette, where we earned a $3,000 flat fee.

> He had been using his jacket as a pillow for his head but it evidentally slipped out from that position while he slept. Barry describes the police officer of having poked around with his entire forebody in the car, leaning over Red Dog before he ultimately found the pills. Red Dog's feet would have been facing towards the police chief, his head away from the police chief and his jacket still further away from the police chief on the rear seat. While this was going on and the sheriff was claiming he was going to arrest Betts and Red Dog, Joe Dan Petty went to the truck and awakened Willie Perkins who came outside and approached the trouble area. After talking to Willie Perkins, the police chief placed Willie and Dickie Betts in his car and told them to remain there. He then placed Red Dog and Barry Oakley in another police car driven by a fellow named Jethro and told them to wait there.

As we left in the rental cars and equipment truck for an overnight drive to college shows in Alabama, I instructed the drivers to take a longer route via Interstate 65 to avoid the back roads of rural Alabama. Exhausted, I drifted off to a deep sleep listening to "In Memory of Elizabeth Reed" on a New Orleans radio station. Unfortunately, our lead vehicle made a wrong turn in Mobile, and I was jolted awake in the early morning by a massive drug bust going down at a roadside restaurant in Grove Hill, near Jackson, Alabama. We were all arrested on various drug-related charges, and each of us was held on $2,000 cash bonds. Roadies Mike Callahan and Kim Payne had luckily missed the trip due to illness. Kim Payne was recovering from having been shot by a Macon police officer. This drug bust was probably the biggest thing to ever happen, before or since, in that small community of Grove Hill.

MARCH 24, 1971

UNIVERSITY OF ALABAMA

TUSCALOOSA, ALABAMA

We were disinvited to a scheduled college show in Montevallo, Alabama, on March 22. No problem, we were still in jail. Finally, bail was posted, and upon release we headed for a concert at the University of Alabama in Tuscaloosa for a flat fee of $4,500. This was after I instructed the band to check their luggage for any further contraband. They did, and promptly consumed all undiscovered contents. We received a surprisingly cordial welcome in Tuscaloosa, but there was no time to relax. We had to perform in St. Paul, Minnesota, the following night.

Attorneys John Condon and Joe Sedita, who had handled the Twiggs Lyndon case in Buffalo, were retained to address the Alabama charges. Eventually, the felony charges against Joe Dan Petty and I were dropped. The State's case was weak because of a legally faulty search, and after no one appeared in court, the cash bond was forfeited and all charges were dropped. This would not be our last contact with the Condon law firm.

MARCH 25, 1971

ST. CATHERINE COLLEGE

ST. PAUL, MINNESOTA

The band wanted to accept every concert offer they could possibly make, so they authorized me to confirm every offer that I determined to be logistically feasible. The fact that we had two separate booking agencies sometimes made it difficult. Walden Artists and Promotions in Macon booked the South, and Associated Booking Corporation, headquartered in New York City, with branch offices nationwide, booked the remainder of the United States.

Because of this, sometimes nightmarish overnight jumps occurred. Later, Paragon Agency in Macon would book the entire United States.

Tuscaloosa, Alabama, to St. Paul, Minnesota, is one thousand miles overnight and a very difficult jump to make. In these situations, a late start, a cancelled or delayed flight, or weather problems could cause us to miss the date. We also had to transport the equipment via airfreight. We drove from Tuscaloosa to Birmingham and then flew to Minneapolis, changing planes in Atlanta. We made it in plenty of time for our concert in the O'Shaughnessy Auditorium at St Catherine College in St. Paul, where we earned a $3,500 flat fee. I was always proud of my planning and execution and the cooperation of the band and crew. They rarely, if ever, complained.

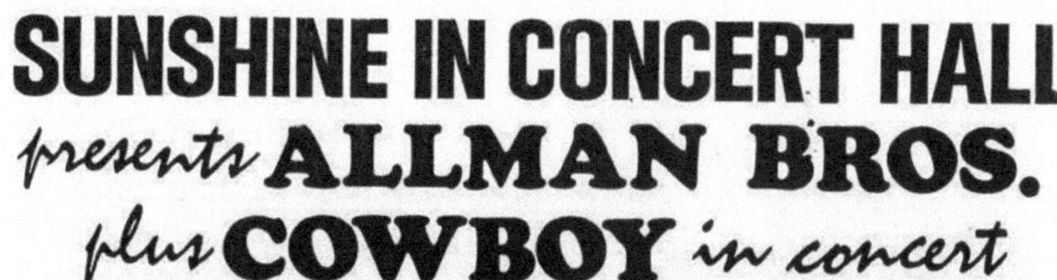

SATURDAY EVE., MARCH 27
TWO SHOWS 7:30 & 10:30 PM
SPECIAL ADDED ATTRACTION
BRUCE SPRINGSTEEN
and Friendly Enemies
TICKETS AVAILABLE AT
SUNSHINE IN BOX OFFICE FIRST AVE.& KINGSLEY AVE. ASBURY PARK N.
TELEPHONE 775-6876 775-6864 OPEN 24 HOURS

MARCH 27, 1971

SUNSHINE IN CONCERT HALL

ASBURY PARK, NEW JERSEY

We had the luxury of a travel day after St. Paul. The band and equipment flew to Philadelphia and then drove to Asbury Park, New Jersey. Our equipment truck was driven up empty from Alabama to join us.

We earned $5,000 performing at the Sunshine In Concert Hall with Cowboy and a young local artist, Bruce Springsteen. Much more would be heard from him later. We had five days off before resuming our busy touring schedule right back in New Jersey.

APRIL 9, 1971

MACON COLISEUM

MACON, GEORGIA

April 1971 was yet another busy month for The Allman Brothers Band. We played concerts in seventeen cities in twelve states, grossing approximately $74,000, for a per-show average of about $4,350. Duane was especially encouraged by our progress and let everyone know about it.

On April 9, we headlined Macon's largest venue, the Macon Coliseum, with Cowboy opening. The Coliseum was built in 1968 and held about 9,000 for concerts at that time. The band earned a guarantee of $5,000 plus $693 in performance overage bonus. Of course, there were no travel expenses involved.

LEADER Duane Allman
TO CONSIST OF Six (6)
DATE(S) OF ENGAGEMENT April 9, 1971
TERMS 5000 plus 60% of gross over...
DEPOSIT 2500
HOURS OF EMPLOYMENT 1 Show - TBA
Concert - beginning at 8pm
REHEARSAL
LOCATION Coliseum
STREET
CITY/STATE Macon, Ga.
TELEPHONE(S)

MAY 1, 1971

UNIVERSITY OF NORTH CAROLINA

CHAPEL HILL, NORTH CAROLINA

We ended the month of April with a concert at the Muskingum College Gym in New Concord, Ohio, for $5,000 and then made an overnight jump to Chapel Hill, North Carolina, to perform at the University of North Carolina's annual Jubilee event.

The Allman Brothers Band headlined an evening show for $5,500 with supporting acts Muddy Waters, J. Geils Band, and Alex Taylor. It was a great lineup. Afterwards, we loaded out quickly and rushed the equipment truck on the road for a five hundred-mile overnight jump to New York City. We had two separate shows there the next day.

MAY 2, 1971

CITY COLLEGE OF NEW YORK & HOFSTRA UNIVERSITY

NEW YORK CITY & HEMPSTEAD, NEW YORK

This was another overnight jump where the slightest delay or miscalculation could cause failure, but we arrived on time for a 2 P.M. afternoon concert outdoors at Lewisohn Stadium at City College of New York. The Youngbloods opened the concert and The Allman Brothers Band headlined for a $6,000 flat fee. Afterwards, we packed up and took the short twenty-mile ride to Hofstra University in Hempstead, New York, where we performed that evening for a flat fee of $4,500. As previously noted, most colleges paid top dollar for student entertainment.

We had earned $21,000 in four venues in three states in three days. Again, it was very difficult but rewarding work. Perhaps the most satisfying aspect was that more and more fans nationwide were seeing and falling in love with the band and their music.

MAY 14, 1971

THE SPECTRUM

PHILADELPHIA

After a well-deserved respite of five days off, we were back on the road again. Days off were not really days off for me. It took a day to get home, and we would normally leave the night before the next show. In between, I had to perform all the accounting work for the previous shows, pay bills, and prepare for the next run. It took a toll on my nerves and my marriage, and I was divorced in 1974.

We played four shows in Tennessee and one in Mississippi before heading north again to the Spectrum in Philadelphia. The Allman Brothers Band had equal billing and co-headlined with Johnny Winter, who closed the show. Special Guest Redbone opened. We received a $5,000 fee.

MAY 15, 1971

SKIDMORE COLLEGE

SARATOGA SPRINGS, NEW YORK

We overnighted up to Saratoga Springs, New York, for a concert at Skidmore College. Admission was free at an outdoor concert for which the band received a $5,000 flat fee. As I recall, this was an especially hot performance by the band. These lucrative college shows helped our ever-increasingly profitable operations.

Friend and photographer Kathy Hurley took some really great photos at this show. They are widely seen on band fan sites on Facebook.

MAY 26, 1971

MILE HIGH RACEWAY

BOULDER, COLORADO

Occasionally, a novice promoter would make us an offer we could not refuse. Such was the case when we were offered $10,000, paid in full and in advance, to fly out to Boulder, Colorado, for a concert. Delaney and Bonnie & Friends headlined outdoors at the Mile High Raceway in nearby Lafayette, Colorado. Several other bands also appeared. The Allman Brothers Band flew in, performed, and flew home. We would gross another $72,500 for the month of May.

JUNE 25–27, 1971

FILLMORE EAST

NEW YORK, NEW YORK

We were shocked and disappointed to learn that Bill Graham was closing the Fillmore East in New York City. He simply could no longer compete with offers bands were receiving from other promoters at larger venues in the city, so he simply decided to shut down. However, we were honored he chose The Allman Brothers Band to headline the final shows.

BILL GRAHAM AND THE FILLMORE EAST FAMILY
INVITE YOU TO
THE FINAL FILLMORE EAST EVENING
A CONCERT CELEBRATION
WITH
ALLMAN BROTHERS BAND
J. GEILS BAND
JOE'S LIGHTS
Special Guest Artists & Jams
Food, Drink & Joy
SUNDAY, JUNE 27 — 8:00 P. M.

Admission only with complimentary ticket(s) enclosed.

Important: Please read reverse side.

The Friday- and Saturday-night shows featuring Albert King and the J. Geils Band sold out, earning The Allman Brothers Band a guarantee of $7,500 plus a bonus overage fee of $5,296.50. An invitation-only Sunday-night closing event added Country Joe, Mountain, Edgar Winter and White Trash, and the Beach Boys to the bill. New York City's premier FM rock stations WNEW and WPLJ simulcast the concert live. The Beach Boys threatened to pack up and walk out if not allowed to close the show, but Bill Graham insisted that The Allman Brothers Band would close, and the Beach Boys settled for an earlier time slot. It was a very long evening, and The Allman Brothers Band was worn out from the long weekend when they finally took the stage. Their set, while good, did not top the Friday and Saturday shows.

I had always admired Bill Graham's dual time zone analog watch, so I went out and bought myself one. It was the end of an era in New York City rock and roll history.

JULY 17, 1971

MUNICIPAL AUDITORIUM

ATLANTA

We had a fairly light schedule in July. The constant touring was taking a toll on everyone, but we would soon return to full speed ahead. I had begun to notice that drug use among the band and other crew members was increasing. Duane Allman warned me to never try heroin, and I never have, to this day.

New York promoter Howard Stein ventured into Atlanta, and we played two shows for him at Atlanta's Municipal Auditorium on July 17. The Hampton Grease Band opened the afternoon concert, and the evening show was opened by Cowboy. We experimented with our payoff terms and earned a healthy $15,590, although we never used that exact formula again. Determining the contractual guarantee and percentage overage bonus is a highly exact and technical process dependent on many factors, including ticket price, venue size, production expense, venue rental fee, police/security, sound and lights, and much more. The correct formula will produce a near or complete sellout with a profit for the promoter and a much larger profit for the artist. The artist's personal management and booking agents work closely together in negotiating the best possible terms for the artist in each situation. Our policy was to "put an ass on every seat."

AUGUST 17, 1971

BOSTON COMMON

BOSTON

Boston Common is the oldest public park in America, covering fifty acres of downtown Boston. It originated in 1634. The Allman Brothers Band performed at the Sunset Series of concerts produced by promoter Don Law for the City of Boston. The band received a fee of $6,500, and Wet Willie opened.

Duane Allman led the band in performing a jam version of "Soul Serenade" as a tribute to blues and soul musician King Curtis, who had been killed days earlier in a senseless stabbing. Duane had attended the funeral. I believe J. Geils also sat in on at least one song. A recording of this concert was released in 2007.

The concert was well attended, and the performance was excellent. Personal manager Phil Walden attended, and there was a great sense of camaraderie. Things were going great and our dreams were coming true.

SEPTEMBER 3, 1971

PLACE DES NATIONS

MONTREAL, CANADA

When faced with conflicting offers on successive nights in either Montreal or Miami, we decided to do both back-to-back. It was a very difficult jump involving customs clearance and flying the equipment, but then again it was just another day in the office.

All of us had to have Canadian work permits and an equipment manifest listing every item down to the last drumstick and cable, but we cleared Canadian Customs without incident. The band performed at the Place des Nations for the City of Montreal. Alex Taylor with Friends and Neighbors opened. He had recently signed with Capricorn Records. We earned $7,500.

SEPTEMBER 4, 1971

JAI ALAI FRONTON

MIAMI

Even if you are an American citizen, it is sometimes difficult to reenter your own country from abroad, especially if you are rock musicians during the Nixon Administration. However, everything worked to perfection and we arrived on schedule. I was elated and even had time for a quick nap before showtime.

The band headlined the Miami Jai Alai Fronton for promoter Leas Campbell, earning an $8,500 guarantee and $1,401.12 in performance overage bonus. Wet Willie and Game were the openers.

SEPTEMBER 19, 1971

SUNY STONY BROOK

STONY BROOK, NEW YORK

On September 15, the New York judge presiding over the murder trial of former tour manger Twiggs Lyndon ruled that Twiggs was legally insane at the time of the killing and had him assigned to a New York State mental facility for an indeterminate stay. This was the best result we could have hoped for. It meant Twiggs could earn his release within a reasonable amount of time.

Once again, we performed at the hip campus of SUNY Stony Brook in Stony Brook, New York, earning $6,000. A live recording of the concert was released in 2003, and I believe it contains the only live recorded version of Dickey Betts's "Blue Sky" featuring Duane Allman. We had our biggest month

ASSOCIATED BOOKING CORP.

445 PARK AVENUE, NEW YORK, N. Y. 10022 / (212) 421-5200 / CABLE: STARBOOK, N. Y.

New Yor
Chicago
Beverly H
Miami
Dallas
Las Veg
London

July 23, 197

Mr. Phil Walden
548 Broadway
Macon, Georgia 31201

Dear Phil:

Please do not sign the contract for Monmouth College on the Allman Bros. Band, October 2nd, as it looks as though this period will have to be moved again. My West Coast office has advised me that they wish to get the Allman Bros. Band out to California as soon as possible and as this is the only time that I see possible, we are blocking out September 27 through October 13 (all inclusive) for an Allman Bros. Band West Coast tour. If this meets with your approval, please advise.

Kindest regards.

Sincerely,

JON PODELL

jp/sf

to date, earning $109,832.24 from thirteen shows. Dark clouds loomed on the horizon, though.

OCTOBER 7, 1971

SANTA MONICA CIVIC AUDITORIUM

SANTA MONICA, CALIFORNIA

We began October with a six-city tour of California, New Mexico, and Washington. Normally, two crew members would leave Macon well in advance to drive the equipment out to the far West. Sometimes we would fly the equipment to the first stop and use a rental truck for all the dates before flying it home again from the final city. After shows in San Diego, Las Cruces, and Seattle, we headlined the Santa Monica Civic Auditorium. Cowboy, who had a brand-new album release on Capricorn Records, opened. The Allman Brothers Band earned a $5,000 guarantee plus a $743.68 in performance overage bonus.

OCTOBER 8–9, 1971

SAN FRANCISCO

We headlined Winterland in San Francisco for Bill Graham, earning $10,000. Elvin Bishop and Cowboy were the supporting acts. Winterland was originally a large public ice-skating rink opened in the late 1920s. In 1966, it began hosting rock concerts that were too large for Fillmore West. Capacity was 5,400.

We were accompanied on this tour by writer Grover Lewis and photographer Annie Leibowitz for a feature article in *Rolling Stone* magazine. Lewis portrayed our entire group as basically a pack of semiliterate Southern rednecks. The article captured nothing of the essence of the band and was widely panned. We played one more date in Santa Barbara before returning home to Macon.

OCTOBER 17, 1971

PAINTERS MILL MUSIC FAIR

OWINGS MILL, MARYLAND

After returning to Macon on October 11, we played Pittsburgh on the 15th and Marietta, Ohio, on the 16th. Then we traveled to Owings Mill, Maryland, (outside Baltimore) for a concert at the Painters Mill Music Fair on the 17th. Wet Willie opened and we earned $10,000. I remember the band and crew frantically awaiting a delivery of some contraband from friends driving up from North Carolina.

PARAGON AGENCY
Booking Slip
ABC/BH
DATE ISSUED Sept 24 1971
EMPLOYER(S) Allman Bros.
DATE(S) OF ENGAGEMENT Oct. 17, 1971
TERMS $10,000 + 60%/$22,000
HOURS OF EMPLOYMENT 2 shows 4:30 PM & 8:30 PM
LOCATION Painter's Mill Music Fair
CITY/STATE Baltimore, Md.
SPECIAL INSTRUCTIONS: 2,600 Seating Capacity $30,000 - Gross Potential D.L. 9/ [illegible]

At this point, everyone in the band and crew except for me had a moderate to severe problem with hard drugs and/or alcohol. Duane and others went to the Linwood Bryant Hospital in Buffalo, New York, for detox and treatment. Some, including Dickey Betts and Joe Dan Petty, opted for self-treatment. The results were indeterminate. Duane seemed genuinely improved and refreshed. He visited friend John Hammond in New York City before returning to Macon. The Fillmore East live album was certified for a gold record award on the 25th of October. The band gifted me with an all-expenses-paid trip to the Bahamas with my wife, Sandra. There was so much to look forward to, but, unthinkably, Duane Allman had played his last concert with The Allman Brothers Band.

NOVEMBER 1, 1971

SNOW'S MEMORIAL CHAPEL

MACON, GEORGIA

On Friday evening, October 29, my wife, Sandra, and I had arrived in the Bahamas and were preparing for dinner in our hotel when I received a phone call from Bunky Odom. Duane Allman had been involved in a serious motorcycle accident and was in surgery. Sandra and I sat down to dinner in stunned silence, and I received a second call from Bunky. Duane Allman had passed. I felt like the whole world had collapsed on top of me. The following morning, we flew to Miami and met manager Phil Walden and his wife, Peggy, who had been on a weekend trip to Bimini. We then flew together to Atlanta and on to Macon.

The next few days remain a blur on my memory. Everyone was in shock and grief. Service arrangements and travel plans for friends and family had to be made. I was also in charge of allowing band, crew, family, and selected close friends to view Duane in his casket, which would be closed during the service. The grief, tears, and sobbing were overwhelming. Duane was neatly dressed in a shirt and trousers and at peace. A joint, a slide bottle, and perhaps a silver dollar went with Duane on his journey.

The band played at Duane's service. They were later joined by musicians Dr. John, Delaney Bramlett, Thom Doucette, and others. Gregg Allman played and sang a solo version of "Melissa." Jerry Wexler of Atlantic Records delivered a deeply moving eulogy. It was a roller coaster ride of both pain and joy. To this day, I think and vividly dream of Duane Allman. Like so many geniuses, his star burned brightly and briefly yet remains eternal.

AMERICAN FEDERATION OF MUSICIANS OF THE [partially cut off]
(HEREIN CALLED "FEDERATION")

ASSOCIATED BOOKING CORPORATION

JOE GLASER, President • • Telephone: HA 1-5200

445 PARK AVENUE, NEW YORK, N. Y. 10022

Cont Rec'd. 11/8/71
Cont. Ret. 11/10/71

LOCAL NUMBER ______

THIS CONTRACT for the personal services of musicians on the engagement described below, made this 26th day of October 1971, between the undersigned Purchaser of Music (herein called "Employer") and 5 musicians (including leader). The musicians are engaged severally on the terms and conditions on the face hereof. The leader represents that the musicians already designated have agreed to be bound by said terms and conditions. Each musician yet to be chosen, upon acceptance, shall be bound by said terms and conditions. Each musician may enforce this agreement. The musicians severally agree to render services under the undersigned leader.

1. Name and Address of Place of Engagement: The Dome, C.W. Post College, Greenvale, N.Y.
   Print Name of Band or Group: THE ALLMAN BROTHERS BAND
2. Date(s), starting and finishing time of engagement: Monday, November 22, 1971
   One 90 minute show to commence at 8:00 PM
3. Type of Engagement (specify whether dance, stage show, banquet, etc.): Concert - THE ALLMAN BROTHERS TO RECEIVE HEADLINE BILLING. NO ADVERTISING IN ANY MEDIA OFF CAMPUS. TICKET SALES RESERVED FOR C.W. POST STUDENTS ONLY
4. WAGE AGREED UPON $ $9,000 (nine thousand dollars) flat guaranteed
   (Terms and Amount)
   This wage includes expenses agreed to be reimbursed by the employer in accordance with the attached schedule, or a schedule to be furnished the Employer on or before the date of engagement.
5. Employer will make payments as follows: Payment in full on eveing of engagement ~~prior to~~ at conclusion of performance, in cash, certified check or money order ~~ONLY~~ or school check.
   (Specify when payments are to be made)

Upon request by the Federation or the local in whose jurisdiction the musicians shall perform hereunder, Employer either shall make advance payment hereunder or shall post an appropriate bond.

If the engagement is subject to contribution to the A.F.M. & E.P.W. Pension Welfare Fund, the leader will collect same from the Employer and pay it to the Fund; and the Employer and leader agree to be bound by the Trust Indenture dated October 2, 1959, as amended, relating to services rendered hereunder in the U. S., and by the Agreement and Declaration of Trust dated April 9, 1962, as amended, relating to services rendered hereunder in Canada.

6. The Employer is hereby given an option to extend this agreement for a period of XXXXXX weeks beyond the original term thereof. Said option can be exercised only by written notice from the Employer to the musicians, not later than XXXXXX days prior to the expiration of the original term, and a copy of said notice shall be filed with the Federation local in whose jurisdiction the engagement is to be played.
7. The Employer shall at all times have complete supervision, direction and control over the services of musicians on this engagement and expressly reserves the right to control the manner, means and details of the performance of services by the musicians including the leader as well as the ends to be accomplished. If any musicians have not been chosen upon the signing of this contract, the leader shall, as agent for the Employer and under his instructions, hire such persons and any replacements as are required.
8. The Employer hereby acknowledges his liability to provide workmen's compensation insurance and to pay social security and unemployment insurance taxes if same are applicable to the services to be rendered hereunder.
9. In accordance with the Constitution, By-laws, Rules and Regulations of the Federation, the parties will submit every claim, dispute, controversy or difference involving the musical services arising out of or connected with this contract and the engagement covered thereby for determination by the International Executive Board of the Federation or a similar board of an appropriate local thereof and such determination shall be conclusive, final and binding upon the parties.

Additional Terms and Conditions

The leader shall, as agent of the Employer, enforce disciplinary measures for just cause, and carry out instructions as to selections and manner of performance. The agreement of the musicians to perform is subject to proven detention by sickness, accidents, riots, strikes, epidemics, acts of God, or any other legitimate conditions beyond their control. On behalf of the Employer the leader will distribute the amount received from the Employer to the musicians, including himself as indicated on the opposite side of this contract, or in place thereof on separate memorandum supplied to the Employer at or before the commencement of the employment hereunder and take and turn over to the Employer receipts therefor from each musician, including himself. The amount paid to the leader includes the cost of transportation, which will be reported by the leader to the Employer.

All employees covered by this agreement must be members in good standing of the Federation. However, if the employment provided for hereunder is subject to the Labor-Management Relations Act, 1947, all employees who are members of the Federation when their employment commences hereunder shall be continued in such employment only so long as they continue such membership in good standing. All other employees covered by this agreement, on or before the thirtieth day following the commencement of their employment, or the effective date of this agreement, whichever is later, shall become and continue to be members in good standing of the Federation. The provisions of this paragraph shall not become effective unless and until permitted by applicable law.

To the extent permitted by applicable law, nothing in this contract shall ever be construed so as to interfere with any duty owing by any musician performing hereunder to the Federation pursuant to its Constitution, By-laws, Rules, Regulations and Orders.

(Continued on reverse side)

Rick Calbi ~~Steve Novak~~ - Ass't to Dean of Students
Print Employer's Name

X Rick A. Calbi
Signature of Employer

C.W. Post College
Print Street Address

Greenvale, New York
City State Zip Code

(516) 299-3762
Telephone

Greg ~~Duane~~ Allman (THE ALLMAN BROTHERS BAND)
Print Leader's Name Local No.

X Gregg Allman
Signature of Leader

Print Street Address

City State Zip Code

Jon Podell
Booking Agent

NOVEMBER 22, 1971

C. W. POST COLLEGE

GREENVALE, NEW YORK

Prior to Duane Allman's passing, we had planned to resume touring in mid-November. Now, there was a question if the band would continue or break off into separate ventures. There was never a thought of replacing Duane with another guitarist. Ultimately, it was decided that they would continue as a five-member band with Dickey Betts adding some slide guitar work. A new five-member business partnership was formed, and Duane Allman's estate would continue to receive royalties from his earlier recorded performances.

Just three weeks later, the first concert was held in the Dome at C. W. Post College in Greenvale, New York, for students only. The band received a $9,000 flat fee. It was so strange and heartbreaking to not see Duane at his spot on the stage, but his presence was there and the band played on.

NOVEMBER 25, 1971

CARNEGIE HALL

NEW YORK, NEW YORK

Carnegie Hall in New York City opened in 1891 with a main auditorium seating around 2,800 and two other smaller auditoriums. Over the years, it has hosted concerts by the most prestigious artists in classical, pop, jazz, and rock music. The time-worn joke with several versions tells of a New York City pedestrian asking a sidewalk hipster how to get to Carnegie Hall. The answer: "Practice, man. Practice."

This concert had been booked prior to Duane Allman's passing, and he had been so proud and excited about it. The atmosphere during the band's Carnegie Hall performance was somewhat somber, reverent, and reserved.

The grief of band, crew, and fans was still fresh in everyone's minds. There were two shows that evening, and both were sold out, with the band earning a total of $14,104.56. Wet Willie opened, and I believe guitarist J. Geils sat in on "Stormy Monday" at the second show.

September 7, 1971

CONTRACTS RECEIVED - ABC

~~WET WILLIE - Sept. 18, 1971 - Hara Arena - Dayton, Ohio~~
~~Terms: $500.00~~
~~Deposit: $250.00~~

ALLMAN BROTHERS - Sept. 26, 1971 - Sam Houston Coliseum - Houston, Texas
Terms: $13,000.00 FLAT
Deposit: 50%

COWBOY - Sept. 26, 1971 - Location same as ABB's above.
Terms: $1,000.00
Deposit: 50%

ALLMAN BROTHERS - Oct. 7, 1971 - Civic Center - Santa Monica, California
Terms: $5,000.00 plus 60% over $14,000.00
Deposit: 50%

COWBOY - Oct. 7, 1971 - Location same as ABB's above.
Terms: $750.00
Deposit: 50%

ALLMAN BROTHERS - Oct. 8, 9, 1971 - Winterland - San Francisco, California
Terms: $10,000.00 plus 50% over $28,000.00/To be paid in full to artist

COWBOY - Oct. 8, 9, 1971 - Location same as ABB's above.
Terms: $750.00/To be paid in full to artist

ALLMAN BROTHERS - Nov. 25, 1971 - Carnegie Hall - New York, New York
Terms: Union scale versus 50% of gross receipts in excess of all promoter's costs.

DECEMBER 29, 1971

THE SPECTRUM

PHILADELPHIA

We continued working into December, playing eight cities in eight states. We wanted to end the year with a flourish, visiting some of our favorite venues. A blockbuster concert was held at the Spectrum in Philadelphia on December 29, featuring support from Dr. John and Jerry Lee Lewis. What a great lineup that was! Dickey sat in with Jerry Lee on a couple of songs. Later, he would go out singly and play some dates with Jerry Lee, much to my chagrin because I could not contact him for several days. The Allman Brothers Band received a guarantee of $7,500 plus an incredible overage performance bonus of $15,581. The bonus was double the guarantee! Contrary to some entertainment experts' and executives' opinions, the band's popularity and earning power had not decreased with the passing of Duane Allman.

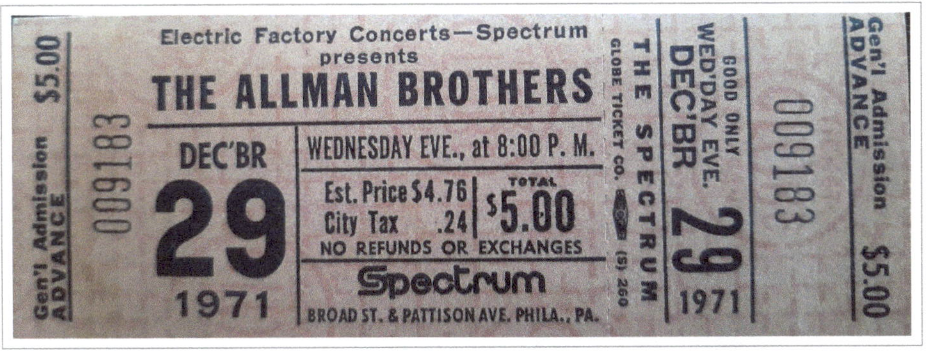

DECEMBER 31, 1971

THE WAREHOUSE

NEW ORLEANS

With heavy hearts but hope for the future, The Allman Brothers Band, family, and friends closed out the year, for the second year in a row, at the Warehouse in New Orleans. The streak continued the following year. Supporting acts were REO Speedwagon and Vince Vance & the Valiants, an oldies group. The band earned a $7,500 guarantee plus a bonus performance overage of $1,963. It was an incredible ending to a year of the highest triumph and the greatest tragedy. The same lineup would perform again the next day January 1, 1972, earning the band an additional $9,000.

PARAGON AGENCY
Booking Slip
Block out
Paragon no ISSUE

DATE ISSUED 12/14/71
DATE DUE 12/21
EMPLOYEE(S) Allman Brothers Band
LEADER Berry Oakley 131 Culver St, Apt. G Macon, Ga. 31204
TO CONSIST OF Five musicians
DATE(S) OF ENGAGEMENT Dec. 31,
overage 1963.00
TERMS 7500/60%/ TBA
To be picked up 17,000
DEPOSIT 3750
HOURS OF EMPLOYMENT Show 1
Concert - TBA
REHEARSAL
LOCATION Warehouse
STREET
CITY/STATE New Orleans, La.

CONTRACT NO. AFM # 485
AFM ☒ AGVA ☐ OTHER ☐
ANOTHER AGENCY ☐
EMPLOYER(S) Bill Johnston c/o Beaver Productions
STREET 1820 Tchoupitoulas
CITY/STATE New Orleans, La. 70130
TELEPHONES (504) 524-1696 891-5345
COMMISSIONS DUE OFFICE
COMMISSIONS DUE EMPLOYEE (12/14/21)
CHARGES
SEND PUBLICITY WITH CONTRACT ☐
HOLD PUBLICITY FOR CONTRACT ☐
SPECIAL INSTRUCTIONS: DR 11/15/71
cont 12/27/71

1972

JANUARY 25, 1972

MUNICIPAL AUDITORIUM

ATLANTA

Going into the year 1972 with the new five-member band raised lots of questions. Early indications were that the popularity and profitability of the band would continue to grow. A new album was soon to be released and a new recording contract signed. Twiggs Lyndon would be released and come back to work as stage manager while I would continue as tour manager. The big question was which, if any, band member would take over the leadership? That would remain an unanswered question for some time.

The first Atlanta concert after Duane Allman's passing was held at Atlanta's Municipal Auditorium on January 25, 1972. It featured Alex Taylor as the opener and was promoted by New Yorker Howard Stein. The Allman Brothers Band received a $10,000 guarantee plus an overage performance bonus of $4,553.

FEBRUARY 11, 1972

CITY AUDITORIUM

MACON, GEORGIA

February 12, 1972, was the release date for The Allman Brothers Band's fourth album, "Eat a Peach." It contained the last live and studio tracks recorded by Duane Allman as well as tracks featuring only the new five-man band. Its beautiful artwork was provided by Jim Flournoy Holmes and W. David Powell. The album was an instant commercial and critical success. It remains on many "best of" album lists to this day.

The first Macon date since Duane Allman's passing was held on February 11, 1972, at the City Auditorium. There were two shows, at 7:30 p.m. and 10:30

p.m., with tickets priced at four and five dollars. The band earned a guarantee of $7,500 plus an overage performance bonus of $4,332.

FEBRUARY 19, 1972

UNIVERSITY OF IOWA

IOWA CITY, IOWA

The band headlined at the University of Iowa Fieldhouse in Iowa City on February 19, 1972, with Big Brother and the Holding Company as the opener. For a time, the fieldhouse was officially known as the Duane Allman Memorial Fieldhouse, which was a pleasant surprise for the band. The band received a $7,500 guarantee plus a huge overage performance bonus of $11,750. For the month of February, we played eleven cities in eight states and Vancouver, British Columbia, Canada, earning $110,207.40.

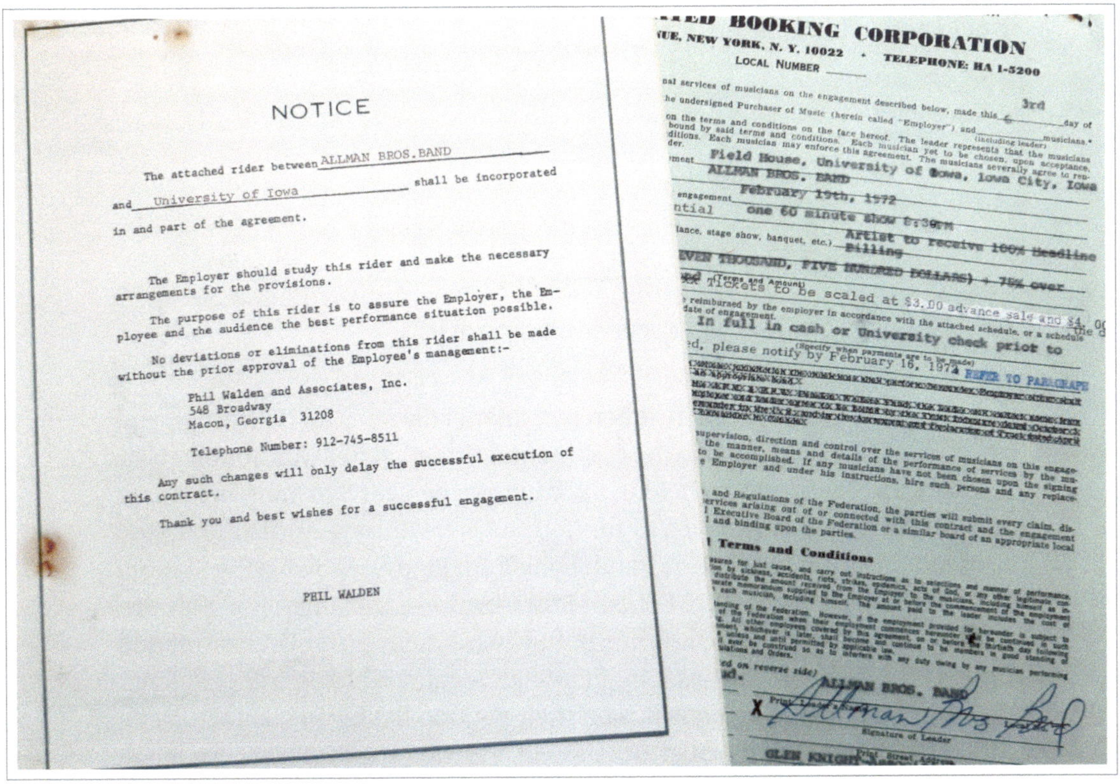

NOTICE

The attached rider between ALLMAN BROS. BAND and University of Iowa shall be incorporated in and part of the agreement.

The Employer should study this rider and make the necessary arrangements for the provisions.

The purpose of this rider is to assure the Employer, the Employee and the audience the best performance situation possible.

No deviations or eliminations from this rider shall be made without the prior approval of the Employee's management:-

Phil Walden and Associates, Inc.
548 Broadway
Macon, Georgia 31208

Telephone Number: 912-745-8511

Any such changes will only delay the successful execution of this contract.

Thank you and best wishes for a successful engagement.

PHIL WALDEN

BOOKING CORPORATION
NEW YORK, N. Y. 10022 • TELEPHONE: HA 1-5200
LOCAL NUMBER

Field House, University of Iowa, Iowa City, Iowa
ALLMAN BROS. BAND
February 19th, 1972
one 60 minute show 8:30PM
Artist to receive 100% Headline Billing
Tickets to be scaled at $3.00 advance sale and $4.00
In full in cash or University check prior to
please notify by February 16, 1972 REFER TO PARAGRAPH

Terms and Conditions

ALLMAN BROS. BAND
Allman Bros Band
Signature of Leader
GLEN KNIGHT

MARCH 3–4, 1972

WINTERLAND

SAN FRANCISCO

Every venue we visited for the first time since Duane Allman's passing welcomed us with dignity and reverence with no loss of enthusiasm for the music. We returned to the far West for concerts in California, Arizona, and Colorado. On March 3 and 4, we headlined Winterland in San Francisco for promoter Bill Graham, with support from Albert King and opener Little John. The band earned a guarantee of $10,000 plus an overage performance bonus of $351.25. For the month, we played twelve cities in eight states, earning $107,878.35. We were on track to earn more than $1 million for the year from concerts alone. Recording, song writing, and public radio airplay royalties would add to total earnings.

APRIL 1, 1972

MAR Y SOL FESTIVAL

MANATI, PUERTO RICO

Outdoor rock festivals were inherently financially risky for both artists and promoters. One held outside the continental United States was doubly risky. The Mar Y Sol Festival was held in the countryside near San Juan, in Manati, Puerto Rico. The festival was to run four days beginning April 1, 1972, and featured The Allman Brothers Band; Long John Baldry; Brownsville Station; Dave Brubeck; Cactus; Alice Cooper; Emerson, Lake & Palmer; Rod Stewart; J. Geils Band; Billy Joel; Dr. John; B. B. King; Mahavishnu Orchestra; and others. The festival was beset by financial, legal, and logistical problems. The Allman Brothers Band was paid their $15,000 flat fee in advance. Actually, we were paid twice in error, and we returned the duplicate payment. A highlight which remains fixed in my mind was our return to our hotel in

San Juan after the show. A helicopter was provided to transport band and crew between the venue and the hotel. By the end of the evening, the pilot had become dangerously fatigued. I put the wives and girlfriends on the last flight out and commandeered a farm truck to ferry the band while the crew packed into the rented-equipment truck. We were a hilarious sight jammed into those two vehicles making our way back to San Juan.

APRIL 14–16, 1972

ACADEMY OF MUSIC

NEW YORK, NEW YORK

I have written elsewhere about how an artist's performance fee is determined, and I will briefly review it here. Artists are paid on a "flat guarantee," a "straight percentage," or a "guarantee plus percentage" basis. A flat guarantee means an artist is paid a guaranteed amount regardless of the box office receipts. A percentage deal means the artist is paid an agreed-upon percentage of the box office receipts. A guarantee plus percentage means the artist receives a guaranteed amount plus a percentage of the box office receipts over a certain amount. All guarantee-plus-percentage deals are individually structured using a complex formula based on the promoter's expenses related to the show, including artist guarantee, venue rental, sound and lighting, security, advertising, etc. An example might be a $10,000 guarantee plus 70 percent of the box office receipts over $30,000. The break point includes all show costs plus a 10 to 15 percent profit for the promoter. Any excess is shared, with the artist receiving 70 percent and the promoter 30 percent.

The deals are negotiated by the artist's manager and booking agent and the promoter. If a show is a sellout or close to it, the artist can receive a huge overage percentage bonus. I conducted the settlement with the promoter in the box office the day of the show. The Allman Brothers Band often received huge overage performance bonuses. As I've stated before, our motto was "an ass on every seat!"

The Allman Brothers Band performed three shows for promoter Howard Stein at the Academy of Music in New York City on April 14, 15, and 16, 1972. Supporting acts were Commander Cody and the New York Rock Ensemble. We received a guarantee of $27,500 plus an overage performance bonus of $27,740 for a very successful weekend.

JUNE 11, 1972

HOFHEINZ PAVILION

HOUSTON

In early June 1972, we embarked on a four-city mini-tour of Texas, playing Odessa, Dallas, Houston, and Corpus Christi. The Houston concert was at Hofheinz Pavilion on June 11, where we earned a $10,000 guarantee plus an overage performance bonus of $5,808.

A typical day on the road began with me waking up in City A preparing to travel to the evening show in City B. I had usually sent the equipment truck and two roadies ahead the night before. If it was a very short jump, the equipment could leave on day of show. I would awaken the band, eat breakfast, and pay the hotel bill. After supervising the bellmen collecting all luggage, we would load up into limos or rental cars for the trip to the airport. Once the band and luggage were checked in and the rental cars returned, we headed to the gate, with the band usually detouring to a nearby bar. Because of the size of our group, we were usually pre-boarded before the other passengers to our first-class seats, where we secured the guitars into their own seat. Upon arriving in City B, we reversed the process and checked into the new hotel. I would check on the progress of the crew load-in and move the band to the venue for a sound check around 4 P.M. Then we would return to the

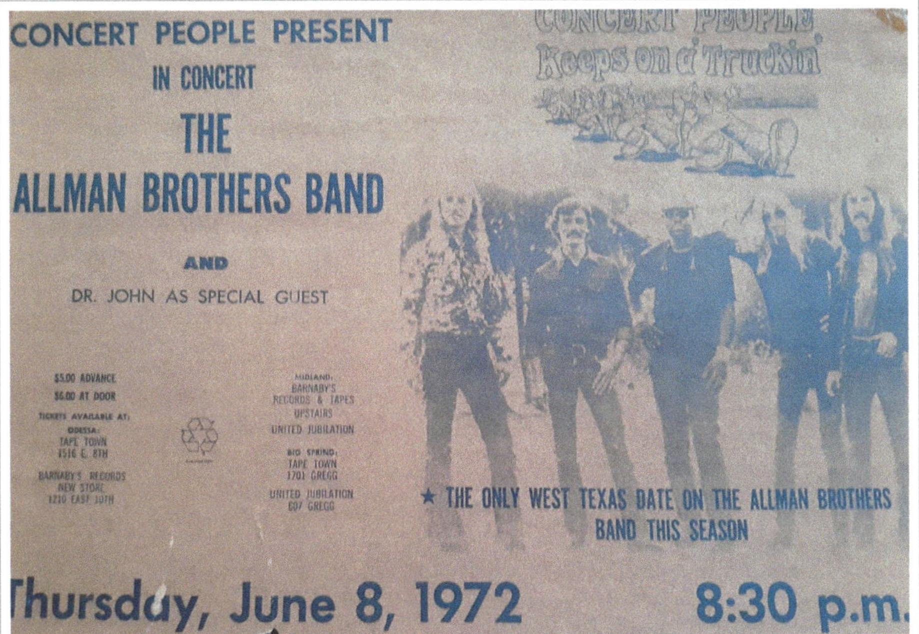

hotel before heading back to the venue for the show. Once the band was on stage and the show began, I would eventually meet the promoter in the box office to calculate and collect the band's earnings. Afterwards, we would usually congregate in the hotel for drinks and female companionship. Sometimes certain band members would venture out to a club or a visit with local friends. The following morning the process would be repeated. At times, I would wake up and have to recall where I was and where we were going.

JUNE 17, 1972

MEMORIAL STADIUM

CHARLOTTE, NORTH CAROLINA

A week later, we were in Charlotte for a big outdoor show at Memorial Stadium. It was hosted by one of my favorite promoters, Cecil Corbett. He owned a nightclub in Myrtle Beach, South Carolina, and promoted shows throughout North and South Carolina. He was a straight shooter and a real character. We made a lot of money with Cecil. The Charlotte show earned us a $10,000 guarantee and a huge overage performance bonus of $13,455.

CONTRACT BLANK Cont. Ret. 6/13/72 **N. Y. S.**

AMERICAN FEDERATION OF MUSICIANS OF THE UNITED STATES AND CANADA

(HEREIN CALLED "FEDERATION")

ASSOCIATED BOOKING CORPORATION

445 PARK AVENUE, NEW YORK, N. Y. 10022 • TELEPHONE: HA 1-5200

LOCAL NUMBER Howard Stein Rider Attached Hereto Nº 11023

THIS CONTRACT for the personal services of musicians on the engagement described below, made this 3rd day of May 19 72 between the undersigned Purchaser of Music (herein called "Employer") and ______ musicians. (including leader)

The musicians are engaged severally on the terms and conditions on the face hereof. The leader represents that the musicians already designated have agreed to be bound by said terms and conditions. Each musician yet to be chosen, upon acceptance, shall be bound by said terms and conditions. Each musician may enforce this agreement. The musicians severally agree to render services under the undersigned leader.

1. Name and Address of Place of Engagement Gaelic Park, New York, N.Y.

Print Name of Band or Group ALLMAN BROTHERS BAND

2. Date(s), starting and finishing time of engagement Tues., ~~June 13~~ JULY 17th, 1972 one show - 8:00 P.M.

ARTIST TO RECEIVE 100% HEADLINE BILLING

3. Type of Engagement (specify whether dance, stage show, banquet, etc.) Concert

20,000 tickets at $5.00

4. WAGE AGREED UPON $ 25,000 (twenty five thousand dollars) vs 60% of gross door receipts, whichever is greater (Terms and Amount)

This wage includes expenses agreed to be reimbursed by the employer in accordance with the attached schedule, or a schedule to be furnished the Employer on or before the date of engagement. (50%) $12,500 (twelve thousand five hundred dollars) deposit due by July 1, 1972 in cash

5. Employer will make payments as follows: cettified check, or money order payable and sent to Associated Booking Cor (Specify when payments are to be made)

Balance due night of engagement upon arrival.

Upon request by the Federation or the local in whose jurisdiction the musicians shall perform hereunder, Employer either shall make advance payment hereunder or shall post an appropriate bond.

If the engagement is subject to contribution to the A.F.M. & E.P.W. Pension Welfare Fund, the leader will collect same from the Employer and pay it to the Fund; and the Employer and leader agree to be bound by the Trust Indenture dated October 2, 1959, as amended, relating to services rendered hereunder in the U. S., and by the Agreement and Declaration of Trust dated April 9, 1962, as amended, relating to services rendered hereunder in Canada.

6. The Employer shall at all times have complete supervision, direction and control over the services of musicians on this engagement and expressly reserves the right to control the manner, means and details of the performance of services by the musicians including the leader as well as the ends to be accomplished. If any musicians have not been chosen upon the signing of this contract, the leader shall, as agent for the Employer and under his instructions, hire such persons and any replacements as are required.

7. The Employer hereby acknowledges his liability to provide workmen's compensation insurance and to pay social security and unemployment insurance taxes if same are applicable to the services to be rendered hereunder.

8. In accordance with the Constitution, By-laws, Rules and Regulations of the Federation, the parties will submit every claim, dispute, controversy or difference involving the musical services arising out of or connected with this contract and the engagement covered thereby for determination by the International Executive Board of the Federation or a similar board of an appropriate local thereof and such determination shall be conclusive, final and binding upon the parties.

Additional Terms and Conditions

The leader shall, as agent of the Employer, enforce disciplinary measures for just cause, and carry out instructions as to selections and manner of performance. The agreement of the musicians to perform is subject to proven detention by sickness, accidents, riots, strikes, epidemics, acts of God, or any other legitimate conditions beyond their control. On behalf of the Employer the leader will distribute the amount received from the Employer to the musicians, including himself as indicated on the opposite side of this contract, or in place thereof on separate memorandum supplied to the Employer at or before the commencement of the employment hereunder and take and turn over to the Employer receipts therefor from each musician, including himself. The amount paid to the leader includes the cost of transportation, which will be reported by the leader to the Employer.

All employees covered by this agreement must be members in good standing of the Federation. However, if the employment provided for hereunder is subject to the Labor-Management Relations Act, 1947, all employees who are members of the Federation when their employment commences hereunder shall be continued in such employment only so long as they continue such membership in good standing. All other employees covered by this agreement, on or before the thirtieth day following the commencement of their employment, or the effective date of this agreement, whichever is later, shall become and continue to be members in good standing of the Federation. The provisions of this paragraph shall not become effective unless and until permitted by applicable law.

To the extent permitted by applicable law, nothing in this contract shall ever be construed so as to interfere with any duty owing by any musician performing hereunder to the Federation pursuant to its Constitution, By-laws, Rules, Regulations and Orders.

(Continued on reverse side)

Howard Stein Enterprises Print Employer's Name	Gregg Allman Print Leader's Name — Local No.
X [signature] Signature of Employer	X [signature] Signature of Leader
1700 Broadway Print Street Address	Leader's Home Address
New York, N.Y. City — State — Zip Code	City — State — Zip Code
Telephone	Jon Podell [signature] Booking Agent — Agreement No.

JUNE 23–24, 1972

JAI ALAI FRONTON

MIAMI

We returned to Miami for a two-day run at the Jai Alai Fronton on June 23 and 24, 1972, promoted by Leas Campbell. The band received a $25,000 guarantee for the engagement.

Berry Oakley was not reacting well to the loss of Duane Allman. He was on a downward spiral of grief fueled by drugs and alcohol. On one occasion, he passed out in the middle of a conversation alone with me in a hotel room. I immediately summoned help, and roadie Kim Payne and I were able to revive him and walk him up and down the hall until he was alert and coherent. Although he was usually able to perform on stage capably, his physical and mental condition would only get worse.

JUNE 29, 1972

CURTIS HIXON HALL

TAMPA, FLORIDA

The Allman Brothers Band played Curtis Hixon Hall in Tampa on June 29, 1972, earning a guarantee of $10,000 plus an overage performance bonus of $8,888.79. We would play one more date in West Palm Beach before returning home to Macon for a week off. I believe Alex Taylor played support for us on all of these Florida shows. For the month of June 1972 the band played nine cities in three states earning a total of $137,417.19.

JULY 21, 1972

CITY PARK STADIUM

NEW ORLEANS

On July 21, 1972, the band played a successful concert outdoors on a baseball field at City Park Stadium in New Orleans. The show was presented by the Warehouse promoters, Beaver Productions. We earned a $12,500 guarantee plus an overage performance bonus of $16,498.20.

Afterwards, we returned to the Marie Antoinette Hotel in the French Quarter and almost immediately all of our room doors were smashed in simultaneously. It was a massive drug bust by the New Orleans Police Department, and most band members and guests were arrested. Many of the crew were still loading out and so were spared. As in Alabama earlier, the police missed more drugs than they found, but it was midmorning the next day before I bailed out everyone and we were able to leave town. Again, our New York attorney, John Condon, came to our rescue. He convinced the district attorney that the search warrants were faulty and all charges were dropped. If I remember correctly, it was Jim Garrison of Kennedy-assassination conspiracy fame. We did make a generous cash under-the-table "good will political honorarium" to an unspecified individual contained in an unmarked envelope passed in the Atlanta airport concourse. Some might say that when the New Orleans police chief received the national "Police Chief of the Year Award" strange New York fingerprints may have been on it...?

JULY 31, 1972

FAIRGROUNDS SPEEDWAY

NASHVILLE, TENNESSEE

We played outdoors again at the Nashville Fairgrounds Speedway on July 31, 1972, to close out the month. Dr. John opened. The band earned a $10,000 guarantee and an overage performance bonus of $11,080.50. It was another huge month as we played eleven cities in eleven states, earning a whopping $236,780.84. The Allman Brothers Band was quickly becoming one of the biggest ticket-selling bands in the nation.

Despite the financial bonanza, all was not well. As the events in New Orleans indicated, drug and alcohol abuse remained rampant, and the earlier detox sessions were long forgotten. I called this the beginning of the "days of wine and neurosis" era, and it would continue mostly unabated for the next four years. Berry Oakley would not have that long as his condition worsened.

AUGUST 4, 1972

COMMUNITY THEATER

BERKLEY, CALIFORNIA

We made a whirlwind three-day trip to the West Coast the first week of August 1972. What would be a major undertaking for some bands was like a trip to the corner convenience store for The Allman Brothers Band. We opened for promoter Bill Graham at the Berkley Community Theater followed by successive nights at the San Diego Sports Arena and the Hollywood Bowl in Los Angeles. The band earned $65,176.97 in guarantees and overages for the three days.

AUGUST 30–31, 1972

MUNICIPAL AUDITORIUM

ATLANTA

The Allman Brothers Band had been a favorite of Atlanta music fans since the days of their free concerts in Piedmont Park beginning in early 1969. The band's concerts in Atlanta had always been hugely successful as their fan base expanded, and they played there one or more times annually. The August concerts at the Municipal Auditorium were opened respectively by Capricorn Records acts Wet Willie and Eric Quincy Tate. We earned $30,000 total from the two shows.

The band would take a touring hiatus in the fall of 1972 for recording and other events. One of those events would throw us all into another tailspin. The next regular concert would not come until December.

July 17, 1972

THE ALLMAN BROTHERS BAND

August 30 & 31, 1972 — Municipal Auditorium/ Atlanta, Georgia

$30,000.00 Flat — $15,000.00

August 1, 1972

15,000.00

Mr. Howard Stein:

SEPTEMBER, OCTOBER, NOVEMBER 1972

VARIOUS PROJECTS/CHANGES

MACON, GEORGIA

The primary reason for the touring hiatus was for recording. Rehearsals immediately began on the fourth studio album, which would become *Brothers and Sisters*. Gregg Allman had some material which did not quite fit The Allman Brothers Band mold, and he also wanted to pursue some different musical directions, so he began to rehearse and record some demos as well. This would ultimately lead to his first solo album release, *Laid Back*. On November 1, 1972, after lengthy negotiations, the five band members signed a new recording agreement with Capricorn Records that provided a $100,000 cash advance, an increased royalty rate from 5 percent of retail to 12 percent of retail, free studio time at Capricorn Studios, and other benefits.

A young keyboardist from Alabama, Chuck Leavell, had recently joined the Macon music scene. His amazing talent was immediately recognized, and he played in the road bands of Alex Taylor and Dr. John, who often opened for The Allman Brothers Band. Chuck rehearsed and recorded on Gregg's solo project and also joined in some studio jams with other Allman Brothers Band members. Eventually, we all gathered with Phil Walden in the Capricorn offices and Chuck was formally invited to join the band. He immediately accepted and we had a six-member band again. In early November, we flew to New York for a one-day television taping of Don Kirshner's *In Concert* for ABC. It would be Chuck's first official performance with the band.

On November 11, Berry Oakley had planned a big show with band members and other musicians at a local nightclub owned by Capricorn Records executive Frank Fenter. That afternoon, I received a call that Berry had been involved in a motorcycle accident. Shortly after arriving at the hospital room, I was notified that he had passed. Poor Berry had never gotten over Duane's death even though he lingered for another year. Lightning had struck The Allman Brothers Band once more. Again, a memorial service was held, and again, the band would play. Berry Oakley would be united with Duane Allman in adjoining graves in Macon's Rose Hill Cemetery. Years later, they would be joined by Gregg Allman and Butch Trucks. Together forever.

There was never a doubt the band would carry on. Rehearsals were held, and Lamar Williams, a friend of Jaimoe's from Mississippi, was hired as bass player. He was a perfect fit.

DECEMBER 9, 1972

CRISLER ARENA

ANN ARBOR, MICHIGAN

The Allman Brothers Band played the thirteen thousand-seat Crisler Arena at the University of Michigan in Ann Arbor on December 10, 1972. Although Chuck Leavell had done a TV taping with the band in November, it was his first concert with Lamar Williams on bass and the first-ever concert without both Duane Allman and Berry Oakley. This six-member lineup would continue until the band's breakup in 1976. The band earned a guarantee of $15,000 plus an overage performance bonus of $12,441.

DECEMBER 27, 1972

HOLLYWOOD, FLORIDA

The band headlined a big outdoor concert in Hollywood, Florida, with support from Johnny and Edgar Winter, the Mahavishnu Orchestra, and others. We earned a $40,000 flat guarantee. By the time the band came on that evening, it had become so unseasonably cold that fans were tearing apart some of the wooden bleacher seats to start bonfires for warmth. It was the coldest I have ever been in Florida.

DECEMBER 29, 1972

THE SPECTRUM

PHILADELPHIA

It was becoming a tradition to play a big show at the Spectrum in Philadelphia between Christmas and New Year's Eve. This year, The Allman Brothers Band headlined with support from Edgar Winter and Wet Willie. It was also a tradition for the band to earn a huge payday there, with a guarantee of $20,000 plus an overage performance bonus of $27,585.26.

1.

A SPECIAL HOLIDAY PERFORMANCE

THE ALLMAN BROTHERS BAND

NEW YEAR'S EVE
SUN. DEC. 31

NEW YEAR'S NIGHT
MON. JAN. 1

WITH

THE ELVIN BISHOP GROUP

ALSO SPECIAL GUEST STARS

THE WET WILLIE BAND

OPEN 8. . SHOW 9
TICKETS: $5.50

If you live out of town and wish to attend these concerts send a money order or money gram payable to Beaver Productions 1820 Tchoupitoulas St. New Orleans, La. 70130. Indicate which day(s) you wish to attend and we will hold your tickets for you at the Warehouse box office. Last Day For Money Orders Dec. 28.

NEW TICKET OUTLETS FOR THE NEW ORLEANS AREA!

Far Out 721 Bourbon St.	525-6923
Far Out 3343 Canal St.	822-9898
Far Out 2026 Metairie rd.	834-9114
General Store 2169 Robert E. Lee	283-4080
General Store 16 Westbank Expressway	366-3130
Red Balloon 615 Canal St.	522-4004
Genesis Records 1607 Milan St. (off St. Chas.)	895-1096
Stash 8735 W. Judge Perez Dr. (Chalmette)	279-4247
Humbug 2705 William Blvd. (Kenner)	729-3339
Budget Tapes & Records 3939 Veterans Hwy.	885-5619
Van's Records 200 E. Judge Perez Dr. (Chalmette)	279-9591

DECEMBER 31, 1972

THE WAREHOUSE

NEW ORLEANS

For the third consecutive and final time, The Allman Brothers Band played the Warehouse in New Orleans on New Year's Eve with support from Elvin Bishop and Wet Willie. The band earned a $7,500 guarantee plus an overage performance bonus of $3,219. Friends and family were there and a great time was had by all. The year ended with a bang, and we were all excited about a new beginning with the band in 1973. We kicked it off by staying over in New Orleans for a second show on New Year's Day, earning an additional guarantee of $7,500 plus an overage performance bonus of $3,060.

1973

JANUARY 12, 1973

JACKSONVILLE, FLORIDA

Jacksonville, Florida, was another city that had always been a hot spot for The Allman Brothers Band. Five of the original members had played with other bands that often performed there, and the original band had formed there after the legendary "Jacksonville Jam" before moving to Macon. Once, when Duane accepted the key to the city from the mayor of Jacksonville after a benefit concert, I told him it must be the backdoor key. That key is still in The Allman Brothers Band Museum at the Big House in Macon. The January 12, 1973, concert was held at the Jacksonville Coliseum, and the band earned $20,000.

JANUARY 19, 1973

UNIVERSITY OF GEORGIA COLISEUM

ATHENS, GEORGIA

Athens, Georgia, home of the University of Georgia, is about ninety miles northeast of Macon, and The Allman Brothers Band headlined at the school coliseum on January 19, 1973, with John Hammond opening solo. The acoustics in that building were not good, but the band gave a spirited performance to a great response. We earned a guarantee of $15,000 and an overage performance bonus of $11,880. We would finish the month with concerts in Knoxville, Tennessee; Cincinnati; Chicago; and Madison, Wisconsin, earning $184,075.35 for the month.

FEBRUARY 24, 1973

LITTLEJOHN COLISEUM

CLEMSON, SOUTH CAROLINA

The Allman Brothers Band had operated as an equal partnership when Duane Allman and Berry Oakley were alive, first as six members, then as five. Now, a corporation, Brothers Properties, Inc., was formed, with shares equally divided between the four remaining original members. The farm property was held under a separate partnership among the original four for tax purposes. Chuck Leavell and Lamar Williams received equal salaries and benefits but were not shareholders. This business structure enabled us to have a pension and profit-sharing plan for all shareholders and employees plus periodic bonuses and other benefits. There were also a medical payments plan, auto allowance, and term life insurance for the musicians plus periodic cash dividends for the shareholders. Unsecured loans were also available to all. It was quite a worker-friendly environment, made possible by the shareholders' generosity and my planning. I was bonded by an indemnity company for around $1 million if I committed any financial malfeasance, which, of course, I never did. At one point Gregg insisted I receive the same base salary as he and the other shareholders, but I declined. There were great tax benefits to this plan, and I am proud to say all of our business and personal tax returns were accepted as filed by the IRS with no penalties.

February 1973 was spent mostly at home in Macon relaxing, rehearsing, writing, and recording. On February 24, we took about a three-hour drive east over to Clemson, South Carolina, to perform at Littlejohn Coliseum on the Clemson University campus. Our old friend Cecil Corbett promoted the concert, and the band earned a $20,000 guarantee plus an overage performance bonus of $8,350. Brother Cecil paid us a lot of overages through the years.

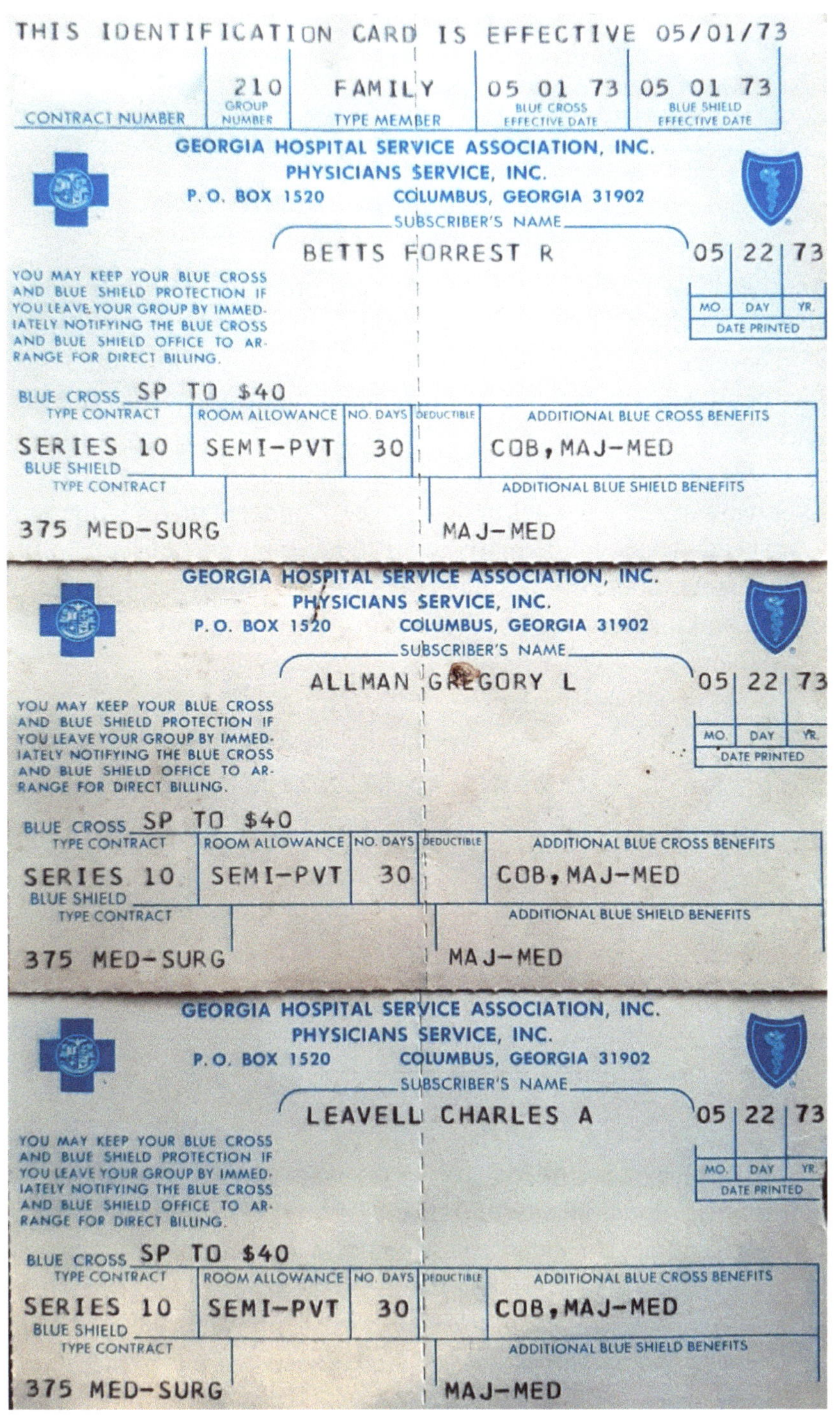

THIS IDENTIFICATION CARD IS EFFECTIVE 05/01/73

CONTRACT NUMBER	GROUP NUMBER	TYPE MEMBER	BLUE CROSS EFFECTIVE DATE	BLUE SHIELD EFFECTIVE DATE
	210	FAMILY	05 01 73	05 01 73

GEORGIA HOSPITAL SERVICE ASSOCIATION, INC.
PHYSICIANS SERVICE, INC.
P. O. BOX 1520 COLUMBUS, GEORGIA 31902

SUBSCRIBER'S NAME: BETTS FORREST R

DATE PRINTED: 05 (MO.) 22 (DAY) 73 (YR.)

YOU MAY KEEP YOUR BLUE CROSS AND BLUE SHIELD PROTECTION IF YOU LEAVE YOUR GROUP BY IMMEDIATELY NOTIFYING THE BLUE CROSS AND BLUE SHIELD OFFICE TO ARRANGE FOR DIRECT BILLING.

BLUE CROSS SP TO $40

TYPE CONTRACT	ROOM ALLOWANCE	NO. DAYS	DEDUCTIBLE	ADDITIONAL BLUE CROSS BENEFITS
SERIES 10	SEMI-PVT	30		COB, MAJ-MED

BLUE SHIELD TYPE CONTRACT		ADDITIONAL BLUE SHIELD BENEFITS
375 MED-SURG		MAJ-MED

GEORGIA HOSPITAL SERVICE ASSOCIATION, INC.
PHYSICIANS SERVICE, INC.
P. O. BOX 1520 COLUMBUS, GEORGIA 31902

SUBSCRIBER'S NAME: ALLMAN GREGORY L

DATE PRINTED: 05 (MO.) 22 (DAY) 73 (YR.)

YOU MAY KEEP YOUR BLUE CROSS AND BLUE SHIELD PROTECTION IF YOU LEAVE YOUR GROUP BY IMMEDIATELY NOTIFYING THE BLUE CROSS AND BLUE SHIELD OFFICE TO ARRANGE FOR DIRECT BILLING.

BLUE CROSS SP TO $40

TYPE CONTRACT	ROOM ALLOWANCE	NO. DAYS	DEDUCTIBLE	ADDITIONAL BLUE CROSS BENEFITS
SERIES 10	SEMI-PVT	30		COB, MAJ-MED

BLUE SHIELD TYPE CONTRACT		ADDITIONAL BLUE SHIELD BENEFITS
375 MED-SURG		MAJ-MED

GEORGIA HOSPITAL SERVICE ASSOCIATION, INC.
PHYSICIANS SERVICE, INC.
P. O. BOX 1520 COLUMBUS, GEORGIA 31902

SUBSCRIBER'S NAME: LEAVELL CHARLES A

DATE PRINTED: 05 (MO.) 22 (DAY) 73 (YR.)

YOU MAY KEEP YOUR BLUE CROSS AND BLUE SHIELD PROTECTION IF YOU LEAVE YOUR GROUP BY IMMEDIATELY NOTIFYING THE BLUE CROSS AND BLUE SHIELD OFFICE TO ARRANGE FOR DIRECT BILLING.

BLUE CROSS SP TO $40

TYPE CONTRACT	ROOM ALLOWANCE	NO. DAYS	DEDUCTIBLE	ADDITIONAL BLUE CROSS BENEFITS
SERIES 10	SEMI-PVT	30		COB, MAJ-MED

BLUE SHIELD TYPE CONTRACT		ADDITIONAL BLUE SHIELD BENEFITS
375 MED-SURG		MAJ-MED

MARCH 17, 1973

MEMORIAL COLISEUM

TUSCALOOSA, ALABAMA

Another benefit provided to The Allman Brothers Band members and crew was a per diem, or daily, cash payment when we traveled. This tax-free stipend covered daily food and incidental expenses. The amount of twenty dollars per day easily covered daily meals in the early 1970s. I have seen individuals use their entire week's per diem to make purchases other than food...if you know what I mean, and I think you do.

After two early March dates in New Haven, Connecticut, and Albany, New York, we headed back south for a concert at the Memorial Coliseum in Tuscaloosa, Alabama, home of the University of Alabama. We earned a $20,000 guarantee and a whopping overage performance bonus of $24,400. Sweet Home Alabama!

MARCH 23–24, 1973

SAM HOUSTON COLISEUM & TARRANT COUNTY CONVENTION CENTER

HOUSTON & FORT WORTH, TEXAS

We next took a quick two-day trip to Texas for concerts at the Sam Houston Coliseum in Houston and the Tarrant County Convention Center in Fort Worth. Combined earnings for the two shows were $76,998 in guarantees and bonuses. The five concerts in March earned a total of $177,252, or a per-show average of $35,450. The Allman Brothers Band continued to be one of the biggest-earning bands on the road. I recall one member of management calling them "ticket-selling SOBs." The new band was performing flawlessly, ticket sales were through the roof, and the cash was rolling in. Seemingly, once again, they had beaten the odds and continued to prosper creatively and financially.

APRIL 30–MAY 1, 1973

NASSAU COLISEUM

UNIONDALE, NEW YORK

The Allman Brothers Band was playing fewer dates but earning more money. In April 1973, we played Charleston, West Virginia; Charlotte, North Carolina; Boston; and Uniondale, New York, earning a total of $210,346.05. The Marshall Tucker Band opened both shows in Uniondale. They were becoming more popular and beginning to sell more records and would become Capricorn Records' second biggest act behind The Allman Brothers Band.

For the Nassau Coliseum dates, we used the rare "90/10" contract formula whereby the band received 90 percent of the concert proceeds after all concert expenses and the promoter the remaining 10 percent. We earned $53,477.91 for the April 30th show and $54,097.33 for a second show the following night of May 1. These were truly staggering earnings.

JUNE 9–10, 1973

JFK STADIUM

WASHINGTON, DC

The Allman Brothers Band co-headlined JFK Stadium on June 9 and 10, 1973, with the Grateful Dead. Caroline Kennedy, daughter of the late President John F. Kennedy (for whom the stadium was named), was one of many backstage guests. It was hot, humid, and uncomfortable, and nerves became frayed due to the huge number of guests of each band, which included some members of the Hells Angels as guests of the Dead. Perhaps due to this, an unpleasant physical altercation broke out between a Capricorn Records employee, Dick Wooley, and members of both road crews and the Angels. Wooley was roughed up quite a bit, and Phil Walden, president of Capricorn Records, was outraged that his employee had been beaten. As a result, the band fired three road-crew members. It was the first crack in the brotherhood and a sad day for all. It was up to me to carry out the terminations.

Critically and financially, the shows were a success, with The Allman Brothers Band earning $101,138.93 total from both shows combined.

JUNE 23, 1973

DILLON STADIUM

HARTFORD, CONNECTICUT

The Allman Brothers Band headlined outdoors at Dillon Stadium in Hartford, Connecticut, on June 23, 1973. Capricorn Records recording artists the Marshall Tucker Band and Grinderswitch were supporting acts. Grinderswitch was led by Joe Dan Petty, former ace Alllman Brothers Band roadie and guitar tech for Dickey Betts. Outdoor shows, with their festival-like atmosphere, most always had a feeling of freedom and excitement. We earned a guarantee of $30,000 and an overage performance of $25,590. At this point and forward, we would be disappointed if an overage performance bonus was not earned.

JULY 20–21, 1973

MADISON SQUARE GARDEN

NEW YORK, NEW YORK

The Allman Brothers Band headlined their first two concerts at Madison Square Garden in New York City on July 20 and 21, 1973. They would return several more times in the ensuing years. "Wasted Words" opened the first show, and the long closing encore featured "Whipping Post" and "Mountain Jam." Quite an evening! The "90/10" contract formula was used again, and $85,626.78 was earned for both nights in total. Madison Square Garden was probably the most expensive venue in the country to work. Another historic concert would follow in just one week.

JULY 28, 1973

GRAND PRIX RACEWAY

WATKINS GLEN, NEW YORK

"Summer Jam: Come Upstate for a Day of Music in the Country." A lot of people responded to that advertising. We had planned multiple outdoor dates with the Grateful Dead for the summer and had already had one successful pairing in June in Washington, DC. We had a final concert planned for later in the year, indoors, on New Year's Eve in San Francisco. In the meantime, promoters Shelly Finkel and Jim Koplik had booked The Allman Brothers Band, The Band, and the Grateful Dead for a one-day event outdoors at the raceway in Watkins Glen, New York. Each band was to receive a flat fee of $117,500 with no percentage bonuses. Bill Graham was paid a $20,000 fee to produce. I will never forget the palm trees he had flown in for a scenic touch backstage. We were notified on Thursday before the Saturday show that approximately 150,000 tickets had been sold in advance, that the event was into profit, and that admission from that point on would be free. We would become the second largest city in New York State, with approximately 600,000 attendees present, by Saturday and would set world-attendance records for a live concert.

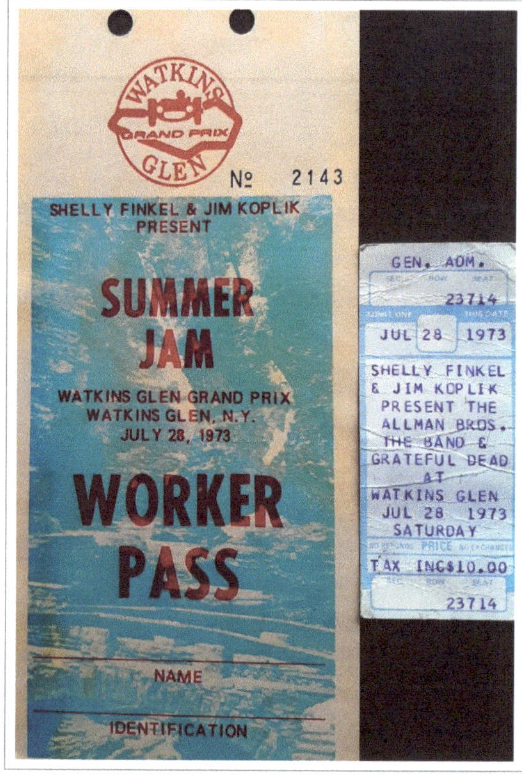

More than 100,000 fans had shown up by midday Friday, and all three bands took sound checks, much to the delight of the gathering. Surely, this would also be a record, as no fans were usually allowed to attend sound checks. Allman Brothers Band personal manager Phil Walden and his management associate, Bunky Odom, held a private meeting in a limo backstage to discuss additional compensation for The Allman Brothers Band. As a result, we received an additional $75,000 payment and, later, a final additional $11,136 from late remote ticket-sales collections. By this time, all ground traffic was gridlocked, and all our travel from our hotel to the venue was by helicopter.

The Allman Brothers Band closed the concert on Saturday with a three-hour set. Members of all three bands jammed in an all-star encore. All 600,000 attendees plus the bands, crew, and support employees left exhausted but happy. It was a great musical, logistical, and financial success with no real hassles or unpleasantness. Only one unfortunate fatality from an unrelated skydiving accident marred an otherwise "Day of Music in the Country."

AUGUST 1973

VARIOUS

We were gearing up for a big album release tour beginning in September 1973, so touring in August was limited. The band played Little Rock, Arkansas; St. Louis, Missouri; and Pittsburgh, earning $86,115.80 in guarantees and overages total for the three shows.

The new studio album, *Brothers and Sisters*, was released during the month. It quickly became a huge seller, ultimately earning both gold- and platinum-certified sales awards. The album went to number one on *Billboard* magazine's best-selling album charts while the emphasis single, "Ramblin' Man," peaked at number two on *Billboard's* best-selling singles chart, topped only by Cher's single "Half-Breed." Critic's reviews were very positive and concert earnings increased again. I can remember walking into the Tower Records store on Sunset Boulevard in Los Angeles and seeing stacks of the albums in their factory cartons displayed at the front of the store. The Allman Brothers Band was now a hugely successful and critically acclaimed enterprise in radio airplay, record sales, and concert ticket sales, but tiny cracks were continuing to spread in its foundation. Drug and alcohol abuse, personal rivalries, creative differences, and financial excesses continued to fester.

PARAGON AGENCY

P. O. BOX 4408, MACON, GEORGIA 31208

Agreement No. 4846

Phone: Area Code (912) 742-3381

THIS CONTRACT for the personal services of musicians on the engagement described below, made this 13th day o September 1973, between the undersigned Purchaser of Music (herein called "Employer") and six(6) (Including leader) musicians. The musicians are engaged severally on the terms and conditions on the face hereof. The leader represents that the musician already designated have agreed to be bound by said terms and conditions. Each musician yet to be chosen, upon acceptance shall be bound by said terms and conditions. Each musician may enforce this agreement. The musicians severally agree to ren der services under the undersigned leader.

1. Name and Address of Place of Engagement Pacific National Exhibition/Vancouver, B.C. Canad

Print Name of Band or Group THE ALLMAN BROTHERS BAND

2. Date(s), starting and finishing time of engagement September 16, 1973

Artist agrees to perform one (1) show beginning 9:30pm. SETUP: 8:00am

3. Type of Engagement (specify whether dance, stage show, banquet, etc.) CONCERT

OTHER ACT ON SHOW: BOZ SCAGGS

4. WAGE AGREED UPON $25,000.00 plus 60% over $60,750.00 /plus 70% over $66,000. /plus 85% over $70,000.00
(Terms and Amount)

This wage includes expenses agreed to be reimbursed by the employer in accordance with the attached schedule, or a schedule to be furnished the Employer on or before the date of engagement.

5. Employer will make payments as follows: SEE ATTACHED RIDER
(Specify when payments are to be made)

(Full payment paid in advance to Paragon Agency

Upon request by the Federation or the local in whose jurisdiction the musicians shall perform hereunder, Employer either shall make advance payment hereunder or shall post an appropriate bond.

If the engagement is subject to contribution to the A.F.M. & E.P.W. Pension Welfare Fund, the leader will collect same from the Employer and pay it to the Fund; and the Employer and leader agree to be bound by the Trust Indenture dated October 2, 1959, as amended, relating to services rendered hereunder in the U. S., and by the Agreement and Declaration of Trust dated April 9, 1962, as amended, relating to services rendered hereunder in Canada.

6. The Employer shall at all times have complete supervision, direction and control over the services of musicians on this engagement and expressly reserves the right to control the manner, means and details of the performance of services by the musicians including the leader as well as the ends to be accomplished. If any musicians have not been chosen upon the signing of this contract, the leader shall, as agent for the Employer and under his instructions, hire such persons and any replacements as are required.

7. In accordance with the Constitution, By-laws, Rules and Regulations of the Federation, the parties will submit every claim, dispute, controversy or difference involving the musical services arising out of or connected with this contract and the engagement covered thereby for determination by the International Executive Board of the Federation or a similar board of an appropriate local thereof and such determination shall be conclusive, final and binding upon the parties.

Deposit to be money order or certified check

Additional Terms and Conditions

The leader shall, as agent of the Employer, enforce disciplinary measures for just cause, and carry out instructions as to selections and manner of performance. The agreement of the musicians to perform is subject to proven detention by sickness, accidents, riots, strikes, epidemics, acts of God, or any other legitimate conditions beyond their control. On behalf of the Employer the leader will distribute the amount received from the Employer to the musicians, including himself as indicated on the opposite side of this contract, or in place thereof on separate memorandum supplied to the Employer at or before the commencement of the employment hereunder and take and turn over to the Employer receipts therefor from each musician, including himself. The amount paid to the leader includes the cost of transportation, which will be reported by the leader to the Employer.

All employees covered by this agreement must be members in good standing of the Federation. However, if the employment provided for hereunder is subject to the Labor-Management Relations Act, 1947, all employees who are members of the Federation when their employment commences hereunder shall be continued in such employment only so long as they continue such membership in good standing. All other employees covered by this agreement, on or before the thirtieth day following the commencement of their employment, or the effective date of this agreement, whichever is later, shall become and continue to be members in good standing of the Federation. The provisions of this paragraph shall not become effective unless and until permitted by applicable law.

To the extent permitted by applicable law, nothing in this contract shall ever be construed so as to interfere with any duty owing by any musician performing hereunder to the Federation pursuant to its Constitution, By-laws, Rules, Regulations and Orders.

(Continued on reverse side)

Mr. Sepp Donahower Employer's Name	BROTHERS PROPERTIES, INC. d/b/a THE ALLMAN BROTHERS BAND
	Gregg Allman — Print Leader's Name — #601 Local No.
X [signature] Signature of Employer	X [signature] Signature of Leader
8380 Melrose Ave., Print Street Address	P.O. Box 5127 Leader's Home Address
Angeles, Calif. 90069 City — State — Zip Code	Macon, Ga. 31208 City — State — Zip Code

SEPTEMBER 16, 1973

PACIFIC COLISEUM

VANCOUVER, BRITISH COLUMBIA, CANADA

In its early history, The Allman Brothers Band rarely performed outside the borders of the United States. During my tenure, I only recall going to Canada a couple of times, and Europe once, in 1974. Because of our appearance and vocation, we always drew extra scrutiny crossing an international border in either direction. I was detained briefly twice until I could prove the cash I was carrying was legally obtained. Amazingly, no drugs or other contraband were ever detected but always seemed to appear after we safely crossed. Even Twiggs Lyndon's occasional, unusual sex toys were not seized.

Our eight-city western tour began in Vancouver, British Columbia, Canada, with a concert at the Pacific Coliseum on September 16, 1973. Vancouver is a beautiful city, and I've enjoyed visiting the area several times since then, including with The Gregg Allman Band in the 1980s. It was a good start for the tour, and we earned a $25,000 USD guarantee and an overage performance bonus of $14,669 USD.

SEPTEMBER 19, 1973

THE FORUM

LOS ANGELES

When Dickey Betts was married to Sandy Blue Sky, a native North American Indian, he took a sincere interest in Indian culture and lifestyle. At his request, we formed a nonprofit foundation, the North American Indian Foundation, or NAIF, to raise money for various Indian causes and projects. The Allman Brothers Band donated their services and performed two benefit concerts in Boston and Los Angeles to raise more than $100,000 for that cause. Only out-of-pocket concert expenses were deducted from the gross proceeds. Later, I and others would disburse the funds as directed at an outing in Canada. The Los Angeles benefit was held at the Forum on September 19, 1973.

NORTH AMERICAN INDIAN FOUNDATION
AT THE FABULOUS FORUM
ALLMAN BROTHERS BAND
A PACIFIC PRESENTATION
WED SEP 19 1973 7:30P $6.50

SEPTEMBER 29, 1973

INTERNATIONAL CITY ARENA

HONOLULU

The Allman Brothers Band took a paid vacation in Hawaii at the conclusion of the western tour. We stayed a few days in Honolulu and performed at the International City Arena, earning a $20,000 guarantee and an overage performance bonus of $1,959.67. Blitzen was the local opener. Bill Graham promoted and set up some activities for us, including a yacht cruise. Poor Gregg got such a severe sunburn on the yacht that he could barely make it onstage to perform.

OCTOBER 7, 1973

NEW JERSEY STATE FAIRGROUNDS

HAMILTON TOWNSHIP, NEW JERSEY

My briefcase was a standard-size business briefcase that I inherited from the incarcerated Twiggs Lyndon when The Allman Brothers Band hired me. Later, I would purchase a newer model. The original had a three-digit combination lock, and it contained the entire band tour operation, which included cash, contracts, itineraries, airline tickets, calculator, and other records and documents. When unattended, I secured it to a sink, toilet, or radiator pipes with police-issue handcuffs. This protected it from anyone who would have attempted to open or snatch and run with it, although a dedicated thief could have easily defeated the handcuffs. It was only left unattended if I was sleeping or momentarily indisposed. Literally millions of dollars of cash and checks passed through that briefcase with no attempt whatsoever by anyone to steal it. You will have to read my earlier book, *No Saints, No Saviors*, to learn about me leaving it in a New York City drugstore while buying slide bottles for Duane Allman. Good luck prevailed when I found it right where I had left it, on the floor at the check-out counter, about twenty minutes later.

"EVER SINCE ROCK BEGAN"

KFXM news OCTOBER 19, 1973

RADIO 59 top thirty

1.	**RAMBLIN' MAN, Allman Brothers Band**	4
2.	That Lady ....Isley Brothers	2
3.	Midnight Train To GA., G. Knight & Pips	5
4.	Angie ....Rolling Stones	8
5.	Higher Ground ....Stevie Wonder	1
6.	Yes We Can Can ....Pointer Sisters	7
7.	Knockin' On Heaven's Door..Bob Dylan	10
8.	Keep On Truckin ......Eddie Kendricks	9
9.	Paper Roses ....Marie Osmond	13
10.	Heartbeat, It's A Lovebeat, DeFranco's	12
11.	Half-Breed ....Cher	3
12.	All I Know ....Garfunkel	15
13.	In The Midnight Hour ..Cross Country	14
14.	Photograph ....Ringo Starr	18
15.	You're Special Part Of Me, Ross, Gaye	20
16.	May Never Pass This Way Again..S & C	19
17.	I've Got A Name ....Jim Croce	26
18.	China Grove ....Doobie Bros.	6
19.	Space Race ....Billy Preston	22
20.	Friends ....Bette Midler	24
21.	Summer (The 1st Time) ..B. Goldsboro	23
22.	Woman From Tokyo ......Deep Purple	25
23.	Just You And Me ....Chicago	28
24.	(A) Raised On Rock .....Elvis Presley	27
24.	(A) For Ol' Times Sake ..Elvis Presley	27
25.	Top Of The World ....Carpenters	29
26.	Let Me In ....The Osmonds	FH
27.	Sweet Understanding Love ..The 4 Tops	30
28.	Jesse ....Roberta Flack	FH
29.	Ooh Baby ....Gilbert O'Sullivan	FH
30.	The Love I Lost ....Harold Smith	FH

future hits

Ecstasy ....Ohio Players
I Won't Last A Day Without You ..Maureen McGovern
Never Let You Go ....Bloodstone
The Most Beautiful Girl ....Charlie Rich
Hello It's Me ....Todd Rundgren
Goodbye Yellow Brick Road ....Elton John

On October 7, 1973, we played an outdoor concert at the New Jersey State Fairgrounds in Hamilton Township for promoter John Scher. The James Montgomery Band opened. This was a makeup date from an earlier postponement due to an injury to drummer Butch Trucks. The estimated attendance of 60,000 almost overwhelmed security and crowd control, and we arrived by helicopter. The band earned a guarantee of $40,000 plus an incredible overage performance bonus of $43,072.04. I could barely close the briefcase because of all the cash stuffed inside.

TICKETRON
ADMIT ONE—SUBJECT TO THE CONDITIONS ON THE BACK HEREOF.
NJ STATE FAIR GROUNDS HAMILTON
JOHN SCHER PRESENTS
ALLMAN BROS BAND
GENERAL ADMISSION
2:00PM SUN OCT 07 1973
TO BE HELD RAIN OR SHINE $5.50

NOVEMBER 11, 1973

METRO SPORTS CENTER

MINNEAPOLIS, MINNESOTA

The Starship was a Boeing 720 commercial airliner converted to a private luxury charter. It was reduced to forty-passenger capacity and luxuriously appointed with a bar, bedroom, shower, sofas, captain's chairs, organ, and faux fireplace. It was originally built to ferry high-roller gamblers from Los Angeles to Las Vegas, but it quickly became the ultimate touring charter for the elite artists of rock. Clients included Led Zeppelin, Elton John, Deep Purple, the Rolling Stones, Bob Dylan, Alice Cooper, and others. It was not cheap to lease. The Allman Brothers Band was offered a trial use returning to Macon from Minneapolis in November 1973.

Welcome to Starship 1, the largest and most luxurious private jet aircraft ever designed for charter use. Inside this four-engine jet transport is a richly private world far removed from ordinary air travel. Every imaginable amenity has been incorporated to carry up to 40 persons in penthouse-like luxury heretofore available only to heads of state.
McCULLOCH

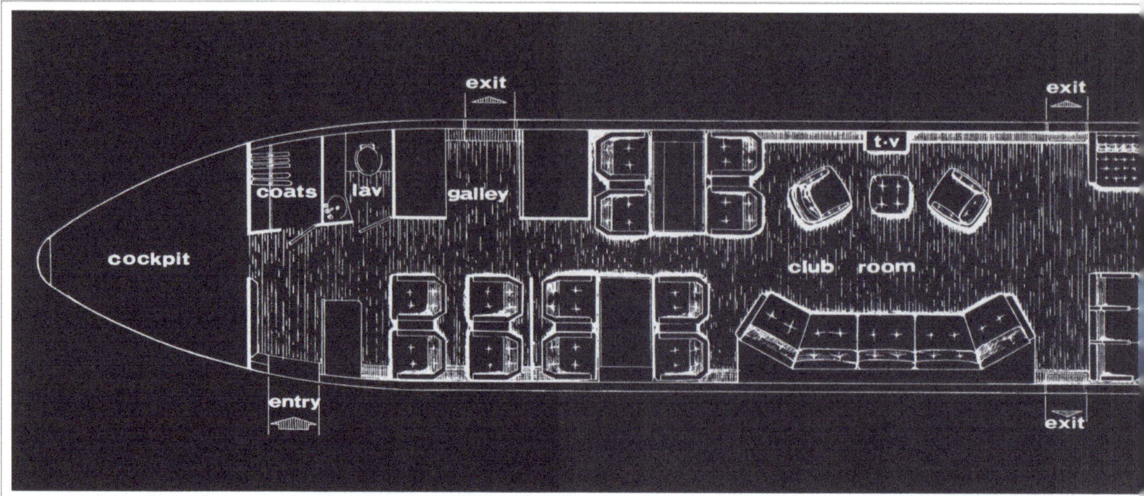
exit
exit
t·v
coats
lav
galley
cockpit
club room
entry
exit

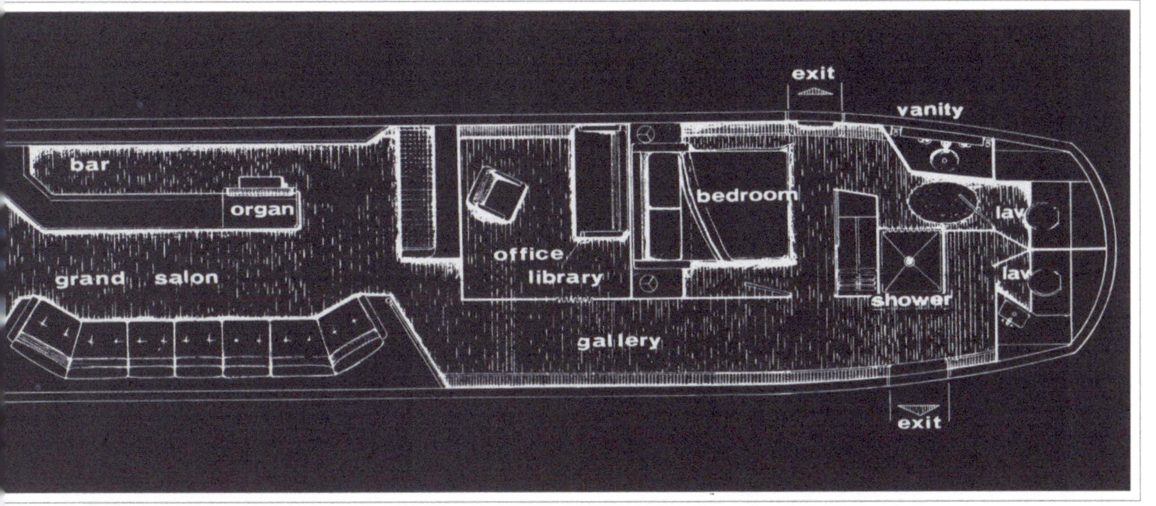
exit
vanity
bar
organ
bedroom
lav
office
library
lav
grand salon
shower
gallery
exit

We played the Metro Sports Center in Minneapolis on November 11, 1973, earning a guarantee of $30,000 and an overage performance bonus of $13,618. Everyone loved the flight home to Macon on the Starship, and we would charter it for the remainder of 1973 and all of the 1974 tour. We were all smitten with the plane and the convenience of no more long treks down airport concourses and baggage carousels. The limos would pick us up at the bottom of the deplaning stairs with our hotel room keys ready and the luggage to follow. Soon we had an advance crew of two who set up all of this before flying commercial to the next city to await our arrival. I was also smitten with a nineteen-year-old flight attendant, Sue Carnel. We remain friends to this day.

NOVEMBER 30, 1973

CAROLINA COLISEUM

COLUMBIA, SOUTH CAROLINA

The Starship charter picked us up in Macon for our November and December 1973 dates. The opening concert was at the 12,400-capacity Carolina Coliseum in Columbia, South Carolina, which had been built as an indoor arena for the University of South Carolina. Cecil Corbett promoted, and The Allman Brothers Band earned a $30,000 guarantee and an overage performance bonus of $3,826.50. As I recall, Dickey Betts brought his pit bull puppy on the road with him. The dog's bathroom habits were not appreciated by hotel housekeeping.

DECEMBER 9, 1973

TAMPA STADIUM

TAMPA, FLORIDA

After two successful concerts at William and Mary College in Williamsburg, Virginia, and in Landover, Maryland, at the brand-new Capital Center, we flew south to Tampa, Florida, and an outdoor event at Tampa Stadium. Sometimes things just do not go well, and this show would be one of those. Cold and rain caused a postponement of the show from December 8 to the 9th. Dickey Betts and Gregg Allman were both rolling, pretty well fueled by drugs and alcohol, and I had my hands full with both of their antics. Bunky Odom of the Walden office was there to help me. It was neither the first nor the last time he would do so. It was still quite cold again on the day of the show and not comfortable for the band, crew, and fans. Gregg was still very erratic, and when I finally got him out of his hotel room and into the limo, we were running very late. I got a police escort to rush us to the venue and get us onstage as quickly as possible. The performance went okay, but it was certainly not one of the band's better performances.

With the kind of money we were making, you want to give the fans your best. Even on a bad day, The Allman Brothers Band sent the vast majority of their fans home very happy. The band earned a guarantee of $75,000 and an overage performance bonus of $26,298.18. Some bands would have been unable or unwilling to perform under the circumstances. I was relieved to get paid and move on. We headed back to Macon and handed the Starship off to Alice Cooper for a few days. The plane's logo and badging had to be changed from The Allman Brothers Band to Alice Cooper and back to The Allman Brothers Band in a matter of days. It's only rock and roll. The Starship would pick us back up for the remaining holiday shows.

DECEMBER 28–29, 1973

THE SPECTRUM

PHILADELPHIA

For the third and final year, we played the Spectrum in Philadelphia for their big holiday shows between Christmas and New Year's Eve. Larry Magid's Electric Factory Concerts promoted two shows on December 28 and 29. Duke Williams and the Extremes and the James Montgomery Band each opened one show. As always, the Philly fans were great. The band received a flat $110,000 for the two shows combined.

The Starship could legally carry only a total of forty passengers, and there were extra family and friends on board for the holiday shows. The band members had promised probably another thirty or so friends a flight to the West Coast on the plane for the San Francisco concerts. Naturally, I had to be the bad cop who sorted it all out and give the news to those unlucky enough to fail to make the cut. Bunky Odom and his companion even volunteered to fly commercial, an unselfish move on his part.

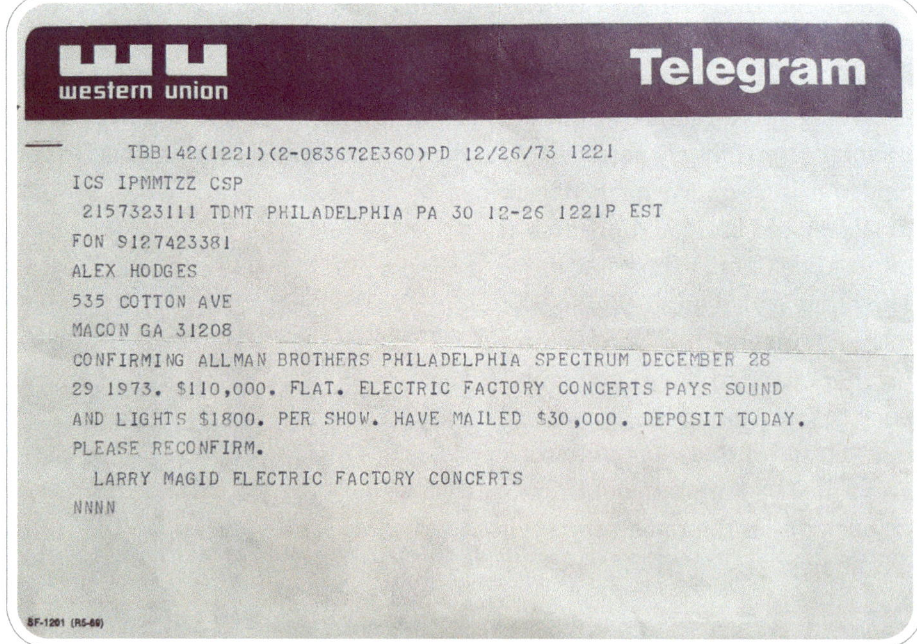

WU western union Telegram

TBB142(1221)(2-083672E360)PD 12/26/73 1221
ICS IPMMTZZ CSP
2157323111 TDMT PHILADELPHIA PA 30 12-26 1221P EST
FON 9127423381
ALEX HODGES
535 COTTON AVE
MACON GA 31208
CONFIRMING ALLMAN BROTHERS PHILADELPHIA SPECTRUM DECEMBER 28 29 1973. $110,000. FLAT. ELECTRIC FACTORY CONCERTS PAYS SOUND AND LIGHTS $1800. PER SHOW. HAVE MAILED $30,000. DEPOSIT TODAY. PLEASE RECONFIRM.
LARRY MAGID ELECTRIC FACTORY CONCERTS
NNNN

SF-1201 (R5-69)

DECEMBER 31, 1973

COW PALACE

SAN FRANCISCO

Promoter Bill Graham hosted his gala New Year's Eve concert/party at the Cow Palace in San Francisco. He emerged from the ceiling as Father Time at midnight West Coast time. The Charlie Daniels Band and the Marshall Tucker Band opened, and Jerry Garcia, Bill Kreutzmann, Boz Scaggs, and others sat in. Drummer Butch Trucks unintentionally took a massive dose of LSD from the Dead Family and was incapacitated for most of the evening. The concert was broadcast live on many FM radio stations across the country via a hookup called the Capricorn Radio Network. We brought in the new year in every different time zone. Everyone had a great time except for possibly Butch. It was truly an evening to remember always. A second show was added on January 1, 1974, with the same openers and Elvin Bishop, John Lee Hooker, Charlie Daniels, Buddy Miles, and others sitting in. There was not quite as much energy as on New Year's Eve, but it was nevertheless another great show as well. The Allman Brothers Band received a flat fee of $80,000 for the two shows combined.

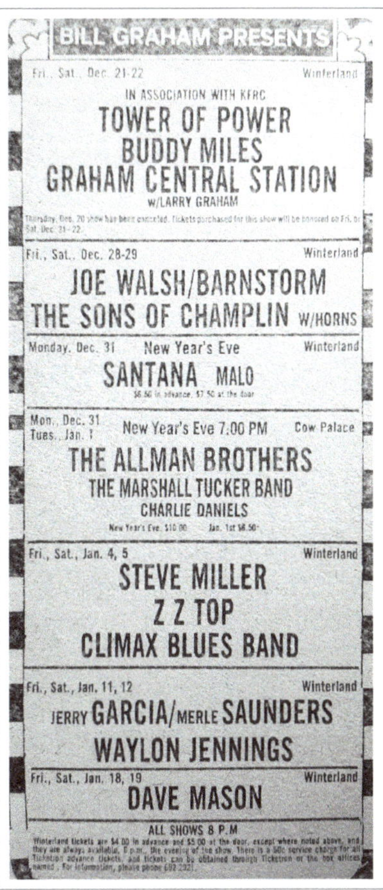

It was another hugely successful year despite the personal excesses, and we would take a hiatus, but 1974 promised to be even bigger, with two solo tours by Gregg Allman, a solo tour by Dickey Betts, and a massive "Summer Campaign '74" by the full band.

1974

MARCH, APRIL 1974

VARIOUS

The Allman Brothers Band would not perform as a unit until late May 1974, but the year would still be very busy and profitable for the brotherhood. Gregg Allman would have two solo tours and record a live album. Dickey Betts would record a solo album and tour solo. And The Allman Brothers Band would have a huge summer tour from late May through August, playing mostly big outdoor stadiums.

Gregg Allman's first solo studio recording, *Laid Back*, was released in October 1973. This album was a complete departure from Gregg's prior work with The Allman Brothers Band. It featured lush arrangements with horns, strings, background singers, and featured songs that would not be a perfect fit for The Allman Brothers Band repertoire. *Laid Back* reached number thirteen on *Billboard* magazine's pop-album chart, and two singles charted as well. The album received a certified gold record award. It was well received by the critics and was a favorite of Gregg's always. It is still revered today and remains a fan favorite as well.

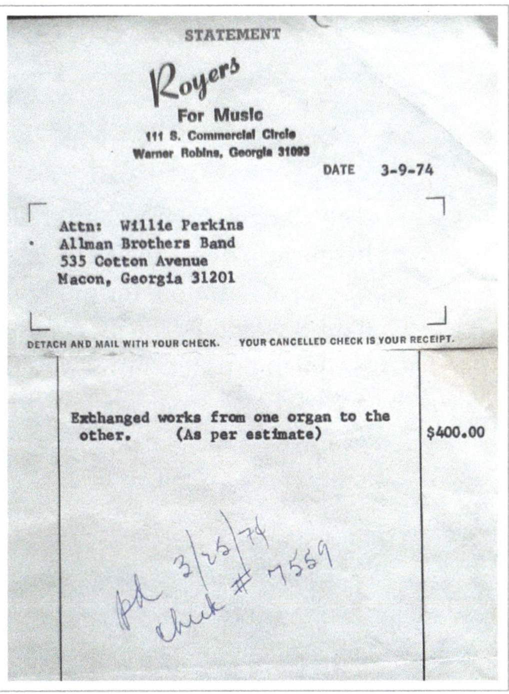
STATEMENT

Royers
For Music
111 S. Commercial Circle
Warner Robins, Georgia 31093

DATE 3-9-74

Attn: Willie Perkins
Allman Brothers Band
535 Cotton Avenue
Macon, Georgia 31201

DETACH AND MAIL WITH YOUR CHECK. YOUR CANCELLED CHECK IS YOUR RECEIPT.

Exchanged works from one organ to the other. (As per estimate) $400.00

Pd 3/25/74
Check # 7559

In early 1974, it was decided that Gregg would tour solo and attempt to recreate the style and sound of the album. Rehearsals soon began at Wesleyan College in Macon. The tour became a massive creative and logistical challenge. It began on March 16, 1974, in Charlotte, North Carolina. We were scheduled to play twenty-six shows in twenty-two cities in thirty-nine days. We had an assemblage of Gregg Allman, a rhythm section, horns, strings, background singers, stage and lighting crew, drivers, a pilot, and other support personnel, totaling about forty people. I was ably assisted by Bunky Odom of the Walden management office and others. It has always been my touring philosophy to hire good people and let them do their jobs with as little interference as possible. For the most part, that has served me well through the years in any endeavor. Gregg and I plus a revolving couple of guest passengers flew in a small private charter plane. Boy, those two guest seats were a coveted prize. Other than drivers in an equipment truck, everyone else traveled on a regular Trailways commercial bus charter, similar to how big orchestras toured in the 1930s and 1940s. It was crowded on the bus, some of the jumps were long, and occasionally tempers flared and nerves frayed. I remember crew member Twiggs Lyndon slept in the overhead luggage rack where he could stretch out a bit. The tour was beautifully staged and performed and was a huge critical and financial success as we returned to Macon in late April. I was mentally and physically exhausted, but there was no time for rest and relaxation as the formidable summer tour by the entire band was a month away.

MAY 24, 1974

GREENSBORO COLISEUM

GREENSBORO, NORTH CAROLINA

The Starship luxury charter picked us up in Macon on the evening of May 23 for the next evening's performance at the Greensboro Coliseum in Greensboro, North Carolina, for promoter Cecil Corbett. Advance tickets were five dollars. It would be the first of nineteen cities, including two in Europe, that The Allman Brothers Band would play that summer. Four cities would each have two shows. In Greensboro, the band earned a guarantee of $35,000 plus an overage performance bonus of $10,547.12. It was a good start to a glorious summer.

JUNE 1974

VARIOUS

June 1974 became known as the "million dollar month," as it was the first time The Allman Brothers Band grossed more than $1 million from concert performances in a calendar month. That equates to about $5.6 million in 2022 dollars. We played twelve shows in nine cities, earning $1,088,364.04 in guarantees and overage performance bonuses. Cities played were Atlanta; Providence, Rhode Island (2); Jersey City, New Jersey (2); New Haven, Connecticut (2); Kansas City, Missouri; Albuquerque, New Mexico; Denver; Dallas; and Houston. Atlanta was phenomenal in that we were guaranteed $100,000 and the overage performance bonus was $133,097.20 with 61,232 fans in attendance at Atlanta-Fulton County Stadium outdoors. The Marshall Tucker Band, Lynyrd Skynyrd, and Grinderswitch supported. Both Gregg Allman and bassist Lamar Williams were dosed with a particularly potent animal tranquilizer, and Lamar was unable to play the first half of the show. Gregg soldiered through, and luckily former roadie Joe Dan Petty of Grinderswitch sat in for Lamar temporarily. Several roadies were detained by the Atlanta police for having pocket knives whose blade length violated a city ordinance. The remaining crew threatened a boycott, putting the continuation of the show in jeopardy until the detainees were released. It also poured rain interminably all through the day until time for the band to perform. Amazingly, the band got a glowing concert review from a noted print journalist, but it was not one of their better shows. It was one of those days when I was very, very happy to collect the huge payday and move on. It could have been a disaster.

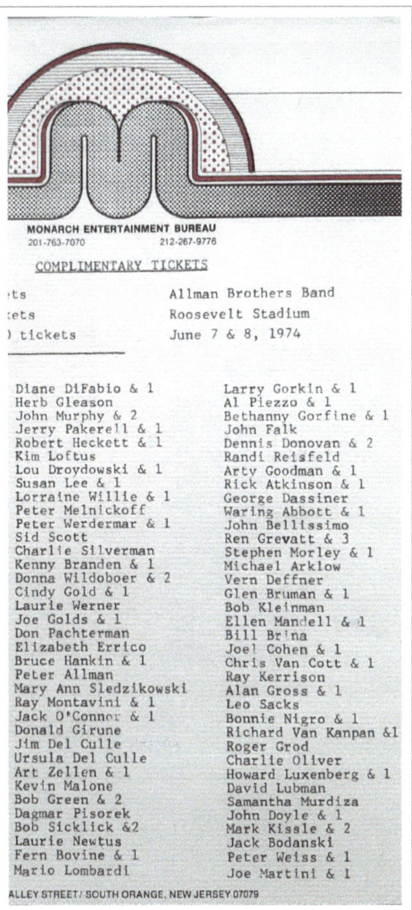

MONARCH ENTERTAINMENT BUREAU
201-763-7070 212-267-9776

COMPLIMENTARY TICKETS

ts	Allman Brothers Band
ets	Roosevelt Stadium
) tickets	June 7 & 8, 1974

Diane DiFabio & 1	Larry Gorkin & 1
Herb Gleason	Al Piezzo & 1
John Murphy & 2	Bethanny Gorfine & 1
Jerry Pakerell & 1	John Falk
Robert Heckett & 1	Dennis Donovan & 2
Kim Loftus	Randi Reisfeld
Lou Droydowski & 1	Arty Goodman & 1
Susan Lee & 1	Rick Atkinson & 1
Lorraine Willie & 1	George Dassiner
Peter Melnickoff	Waring Abbott & 1
Peter Werdermar & 1	John Bellissimo
Sid Scott	Ren Grevatt & 3
Charlie Silverman	Stephen Morley & 1
Kenny Branden & 1	Michael Arklow
Donna Wildoboer & 2	Vern Deffner
Cindy Gold & 1	Glen Bruman & 1
Laurie Werner	Bob Kleinman
Joe Golds & 1	Ellen Mandell & 1
Don Pachterman	Bill Brina
Elizabeth Errico	Joel Cohen & 1
Bruce Hankin & 1	Chris Van Cott & 1
Peter Allman	Ray Kerrison
Mary Ann Sledzikowski	Alan Gross & 1
Ray Montavini & 1	Leo Sacks
Jack O'Connor & 1	Bonnie Nigro & 1
Donald Girune	Richard Van Kanpan &1
Jim Del Culle	Roger Grod
Ursula Del Culle	Charlie Oliver
Art Zellen & 1	Howard Luxenberg & 1
Kevin Malone	David Lubman
Bob Green & 2	Samantha Murdiza
Dagmar Pisorek	John Doyle & 1
Bob Sicklick &2	Mark Kissle & 2
Laurie Newtus	Jack Bodanski
Fern Bovine & 1	Peter Weiss & 1
Mario Lombardi	Joe Martini & 1

ALLEY STREET / SOUTH ORANGE, NEW JERSEY 07079

PHIL WALDEN & ASSOCIATES, Inc.

48 BROADWAY P.O.BOX 5127 MACON, GEORGIA 31208

IN ACCOUNT WITH:

ALLMAN BROTHERS BAND June, 1974

Bookings	Date	Terms	Deposits	Commission	Management
Atlanta, Ga. (D. Curtis)	6/1	100000.00	50,000.00	10,000.00	15,000.00
Overage		133097.20		13,309.72	19,964.58
Providence, R. I. (T. Ruffino)	6/4&5	60000.00	30,000.00	6,000.00	9,000.00
Overage		13385.84		1,338.58	2,007.89
Jersey City, N.J. (J. Scher)	6/7&8	155000.00	50,000.00	15,500.00	23,250.00
Overage		13296.90		1,329.69	1,994.53
New Haven, Conn (J. Koplik)	6/10&11	76000.00	38,000.00	7,600.00	11,400.00
Overage		7500.00		750.00	1,125.00
Kansas City, Mo. (Graham & Fey)	6/14	100000.00	50,000.00	10,000.00	15,000.00
Albuquerque, N.M. (Graham & Fey)	6/20	40000.00	*20,000.00	4,000.00	6,000.00
Denver Colo. (Graham & Fey)	6/23	100000.00	50,000.00	10,000.00	15,000.00
Dallas, Texas (T. Bassett)	6/28	125000.00	62,500.00	12,500.00	18,750.00
Overage		25654.80		2,565.48	3,848.22
Houston, Texas (T. Bassett)	6/30	115000.00	57,500.00	11,500.00	17,250.00
Overage		24429.30		2,442.93	3,664.39
		1088364.04	408,000.00	108,836.40	163,254.60

* Received 7/1/74.

JULY 18, 1974

SPORTPARK

AMSTERDAM, NETHERLANDS

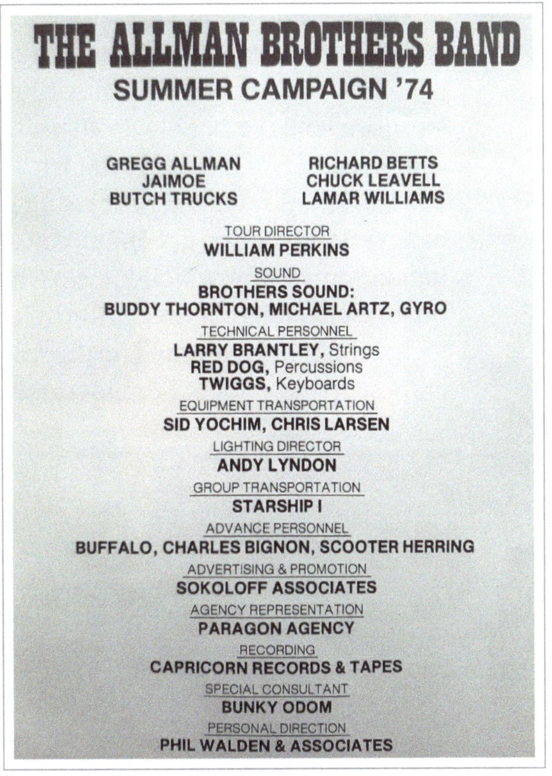

Our first of two European concerts was held outdoors at the Sportpark, about fifteen miles outside Amsterdam in Hilversum. The crew and equipment had arrived a day earlier than the band and me. The local promoter had not properly prepared their work permits so they were delayed in customs for several hours and were not happy when I arrived. The band and I had left New York City in the early evening and arrived the next morning Amsterdam time. Some band members immediately got salary advances to shop for clothes, cameras, and other items. The smoke shops there legally sold almost any substance known to man that could be smoked. The working girls in the legal "red light" district openly advertised their services in window fronts. Although interesting to observe, The Allman Brothers Band and crew had no real need to patronize them if you know what I mean, and I think you do. The local nonprofessional ladies were very receptive to American rock bands.

We co-headlined the concert with the Doobie Brothers and were paid a flat fee of $25,000 USD. Other than losing Gregg's whereabouts for a few scary late-evening hours, the visit was very enjoyable. Amsterdam is a great international city.

JULY 20, 1974

KNEBWORTH PARK

LONDON

The first Bucolic Frolic concert was held in Knebworth Park in the countryside just outside London on July 20, 1974. The Allman Brothers Band was joined by Tim Buckley, the Alex Harvey Band, Mahavishnu Orchestra, Van Morrison, and the Doobie Brothers. It was a great lineup attended by 60,000 concertgoers. We received a flat fee of $35,000 USD. Although we met a lot of musicians, the band did not care for the English cuisine and we quickly flew back to Boston for an upcoming concert benefiting Dickey's North American Indian Foundation. A well-known wife of a very well-known English rock star became enamored of Gregg Allman and followed us home on a subsequent flight. Thankfully, nothing further came of this, and headlines and unpleasantness were avoided. Europe conquered.

AUGUST 10, 1974

CHARLOTTE MOTOR SPEEDWAY

CHARLOTTE, NORTH CAROLINA

The Allman Brothers Band resumed the final leg of the "Summer Campaign '74 Tour" when the Starship again picked us up in Macon on August 9, 1974. The first concert was outdoors at the Charlotte Motor Speedway and featured Grinderswitch; the Marshall Tucker Band; Foghat; Ozark Mountain Daredevils; Black Oak Arkansas; Emerson, Lake & Palmer; and the Eagles in addition to us. Advance tickets were twelve dollars and well worth the price for the huge crowd attending. There were two stages on rails which alternated and kept the setup time between acts at a minimum. Bands and crews were shuttled in and out via helicopters. The concert was a huge creative and financial success, and The Allman Brothers Band earned a $100,000 flat fee. Promoter Cecil Corbett also provided me and our crew generous cash gratuities, which was virtually unheard of. We appreciated it. A few promoters would sometimes gift the stage crew with cocaine to keep them happy and moving.

AUGUST 17, 1974

MIAMI

The Orange Bowl, opened in 1937, was a large outdoor stadium that over the years hosted the annual New Year's Day college football game, five NFL Super Bowl games, and was home to the University of Miami football team. Its approximate capacity in 1974 was 80,000. Even then it showed signs of old age and decay, and the building was finally demolished in 2008.

The concert was billed as Dixie Weekend with advance and day-of-show tickets priced at $7.50 and $10. The advertising poster shows Wet Willie and Tower of Power as support, but Bachman Turner Overdrive was apparently a last-minute substitute for Tower of Power. For some reason, the Orange Bowl was not a popular venue for rock shows that summer. This concert and a prior one featuring some huge acts did not do well. There was some confusion and delay on getting paid the remainder of our $90,000 guarantee, but we did not get shorted. We had received a $50,000 advance deposit, and the balance of $40,000 due day of show was collected. This concert was neither a critical or financial success for the promoters.

AUGUST 24, 1974

LADD MEMORIAL STADIUM

MOBILE, ALABAMA

The last summer tour date for The Allman Brothers Band was outdoors at Ladd Stadium in Mobile, Alabama, on August 24, 1974. The concert, promoted by New Orleans-based Warehouse promoters Beaver Productions, was billed as the Gulf Coast Summer Jam and was unofficially hosted by hometown favorites Wet Willie. We earned $100,000.

The twenty-three concerts of Summer Campaign '74 were a financial and creative success averaging $75,000 per show for a gross of $1,733,214.30. Remember, these are 1974 dollars. Drug, alcohol, financial excesses, and internal creative problems continued to fester, and it was time for a new album. The band would not perform again as a unit until August 31, 1975, a full year later. But wait, there's more!

FALL 1974

VARIOUS

In September 1974, Dickey Betts's *Highway Call* album was released. It had been recorded earlier in the year and was country flavored and roots related. The album was moderately successful and peaked at number nineteen in the

Billboard magazine pop-album chart. A fall coast-to-coast album tour was billed as Richard Betts—An American Music Show. Dickey had requested this billing, and I always felt it caused some confusion in the marketplace among some concertgoers. Fans were familiar with Dickey Betts of The Allman Brothers Band but not so much Richard Betts—An American Music Show. I think Dickey also felt some possible resentment that Gregg Allman was getting the better production and promotional support. I felt Dickey was trying to show the connection between traditional country music and jazz to modern rock music, and it was a great idea. Today it would be called Americana music, and some of the concerts were amazingly powerful. I was given the assignment to be Dickey's tour manager because it was felt I could better deal with his personality and temperament. He and his large band

were indeed a handful, and there were a lot of problems during the tour that caused me much distress. Larry Brantley, Mike Artz, and Andy Lyndon from our regular crew handled production, sound, and lighting. We did mostly fair to mediocre business in many venues, but we finished the tour in one piece. It was a moderate success at best.

A live album from Gregg Allman's first tour in the spring was recorded at Carnegie Hall in New York City and the Capitol Theatre in Passaic, New Jersey, and released in October 1974. It peaked at number fifty on the *Billboard* magazine pop-album chart. A second, slimmed-down version of his first tour went out again without a string section to play some new markets. Due to my being out with Dickey Betts, Scooter Herring was tour manager, with Chank Middleton as his and Gregg's assistant. Jaimoe, Chuck Leavell, and Lamar Williams from The Allman Brothers Band moved over for this tour. Cowboy, a horn section and two female background singers were also included. Twiggs Lyndon, Red Dog, and Buddy Thornton from our regular crew handled production and sound, and an outside lighting company, Concert Guild, was employed. Earl Simms, also from the regular crew, handled transportation and advance while Alex Hodges, Bunky Odom, and I were special consultants. This was Scooter Herring's first stint as a tour manager, and he handled his responsibilities reasonably well. Of course, there was a lot of drug and alcohol abuse, but the shows got played, and the money tally was not perfect, but close enough. Scooter and I often consulted via late-night phone conversations from our hotel rooms. Gregg's second tour was also a success, and both bands finished up in December. We were battered and bruised and returned to Macon for a long and much-needed hiatus.

1975

JANUARY–AUGUST 1975

CAPRICORN STUDIOS

MACON, GEORGIA

Unlike many bands, when The Allman Brothers Band took time off from concert tours, all band and crew members received full pay. This was a very generous policy, but with a weekly payroll of more than $10,000 plus other recurring expenses, cash was flying out the door. I still maintained a full work schedule running the office, paying bills, and taking care of the band members' personal needs. It was time for a new studio album, but the creative juices had just about run dry, and the band members were often at each others' throats. It was difficult to even get all six band members together at one time in the studio. Gregg was now dating Cher, and they would be married in June, only to separate nine days later and then reconcile after Gregg went into drug treatment. Gregg would later record all his vocals in Los Angeles by himself with producer Johnny Sandlin. Dickey's marriage to Sandy Blue Sky would end in divorce and he would later marry Cher's personal assistant, Paulette Ezhazarian.

The resultant album, *Win, Lose or Draw*, was released in August 1975. To be charitable, it was uninspired and received only lukewarm reviews and fan acceptance. It did earn a certified gold record-sales award and peaked at number five on the *Billboard* magazine 200 album chart. Some joked it shipped platinum and came back gold in unsold returned albums. It was a major disappointment for the band and label.

AUGUST 31, 1975

THE SUPERDOME

NEW ORLEANS

The Allman Brothers Band began their album promotion tour at New Orleans's massive new indoor stadium, the Superdome. The supporting bands were Wet Willie, the Charlie Daniels Band, and the Marshall Tucker Band. This was one of four opening events held at the stadium. The others were Bob Hope, an R&B/soul concert, a college football game, and the Ringling Brothers Barnum & Bailey Circus. We earned a $125,000 guarantee plus an overage performance bonus of $44,724.98. It was an encouraging opening date, but we suspected some box office irregularities from the building management, not the promoter. I'm confident there were some unreported and unauthorized under-the-table ticket sales. A lawsuit was filed but never went to trial, and we did not collect any additional money.

This document will confirm the agreement between, Brothers Properties, Inc. d/b/a The Allman Brothers Band, an independent contractor and PACE Management Corporation regarding the sound and lighting necessary for "The Rock Concert" in the Louisiana Superdome August 31,1975.

In consideration for a fee of $13,000 you agreed to provide the equipment, services and personnel needed within the conditions as follows:

1. All requirements in the areas of sound and lighting for the performances of The Allman Brothers Band, Wet Willie, The Marshall Tucker Band and The Charlie Daniels Band in the Superdome on August 31,1975. Said requirements in these areas include but are not limited to sound, P.A. and stage lighting.

2. As an independent contractor you agree to either provide PACE Management with (a) a certificate of insurance covering your employees and other personnel working for you and meeting the requirements of workmen's compensation laws in the State of Louisiana, or (b) you agree to waiver any claims.

3. It is agreed that you recognize the unique circumstances encompassing the problems inherent in the multiple activities of "The Grand Opening of the Superdome." Such problems include but are not limited to the Hollywood Gala to be held on August 29 and the New Orleans Saints NFL Football Game on August 30. These events will require inevitable adjustments in the normal "set up schedule."

4. PACE Management Corporation agrees to use its best efforts to make available all facilities at the earliest possible time after the football game on August 30,1975.

Your signature below signifies your approval of this agreement.

Charles H. Rohe
PACE Management Corporation

Agreed and accepted
Brothers Properties, Inc.
d/b/a The Allman Brothers Band

By:
William Perkins,
Secretary-Treasurer

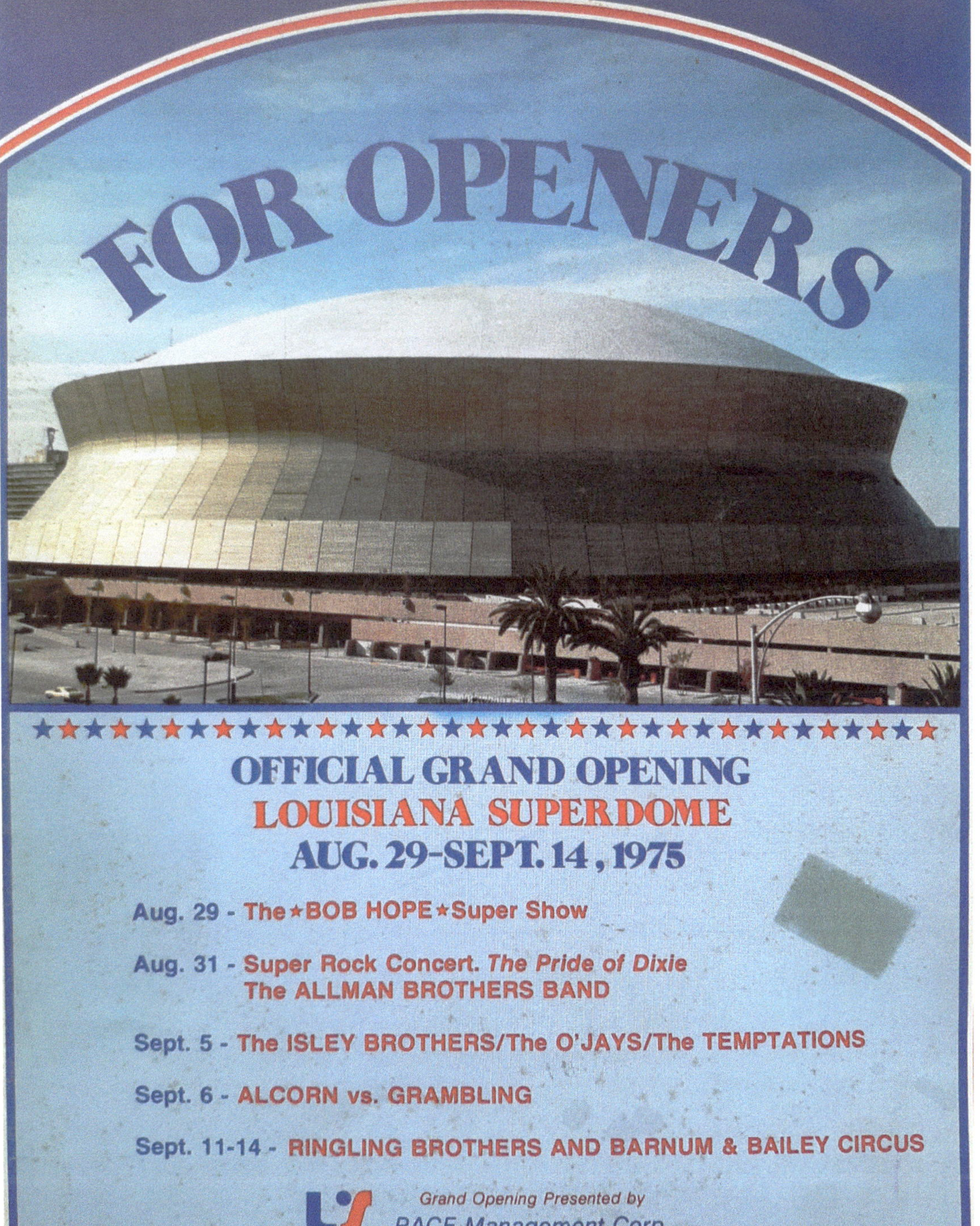
FOR OPENERS
OFFICIAL GRAND OPENING
LOUISIANA SUPERDOME
AUG. 29-SEPT. 14, 1975
Aug. 29 - The ★ BOB HOPE ★ Super Show
Aug. 31 - Super Rock Concert. The Pride of Dixie
The ALLMAN BROTHERS BAND
Sept. 5 - The ISLEY BROTHERS/The O'JAYS/The TEMPTATIONS
Sept. 6 - ALCORN vs. GRAMBLING
Sept. 11-14 - RINGLING BROTHERS AND BARNUM & BAILEY CIRCUS
Grand Opening Presented by
PACE Management Corp.

177 Valley Street
South Orange, N. J. 07079

ALLMAN BROS. BAND		ROOSEVELT STADIUM	
SHOW		LOCATION	
SEPTEMBER 13, 1975		JERSEY CITY, NEW JERSEY	
DATE		CITY & STATE	

	($7.14 & 36¢)	$8.10 & 40¢)		
SHOW #1	$7.50	$ 8.50	$	
Start	21,272	4,346		
End	0	64		
Total Sold	21,272	4,282		
Less Comps	550*	0		*300 1% comps
Net Sold	20,722	4,282		250 J.C. Awake
GROSS	$155,415.00	$ 36,397.00	$	$191,812.00 TOTAL

SHOW #2	$	$	$	
Start				
End				
Total Sold				
Less Comps				
Net Sold				
GROSS	$	$	$	$ TOTAL

Show #1	
Show #2	
TOTAL GROSS	191,812.00
Less 5% Tax	9,172.72
TOTAL NET	182,639.28
Less Overage	180,000.00
% Figure	2,639.28
60% Due Group	1,583.56
Plus Guarantee	75,000.00
TOTAL DUE GROUP	76,583.56
Less Deposit	37,500.00
TOTAL BALANCE	39,083.56

Cash $ 10,000.00
Check 29,083.56
39,083.56

FOR MONARCH ENTERTAINMENT

FOR THE GROUP

SEPTEMBER 13, 1975

ROOSEVELT STADIUM

JERSEY CITY, NEW JERSEY

We were no longer in the Starship charter, but in a smaller, less expensive plane. We still had a large crew and traveling party. I think some, including myself, had an inkling this might possibly be the last tour. Around this time there was also a cover story in *People* magazine about Gregg and Cher but with little about the band itself. It was not particularly well received by the other band members. We were constantly plagued by pushy British reporters from the *National Inquirer*, and I had to assign an additional crew member to facilitate Gregg and Cher's public movements. We had opened September with five concerts in major and secondary markets, and concert attendance was good to average. On September 13, 1975, we performed outdoors at Roosevelt Stadium in Jersey City, New Jersey, for promoter John Scher. The band earned a nice guarantee of $75,000, but only a small overage performance bonus of $1,583.56.

PERKINS MR W. (NO INFO) 3/16
1/INCD. 9/12/75 (920) JP/MM
SHIP & SHORE TRAVEL GROUP
657 WALNUT ST., MACON GA

St. Moritz
ON THE PARK NEW YORK

MEMO		DATE	EXPLANATION	AMT. CHARGED	AMT. CREDITED	BAL. DUE
	1	SEP13-75	RESTR	* 10.00		* 10.00
	2	SEP13-75	RESTR	* 9.00		* 19.00
	3	SEP15-75				* 19.00
	4	SEP15-75	L'DIST	* 0.42		
	5	SEP15-75	L'DIST	* 0.37		
	6	SEP15-75	L'DIST	* 2.08		* 21.87
	7	SEP14-75				* 21.87
	8	SEP14-75	L'DIST	* 2.09		* 23.96
	9	SEP15-75				* 23.96
	10	SEP15-75	L'DIST	* 3.05		
	11	SEP15-75	L'DIST	* 1.93		
	12	SEP15-75	L'DIST	* 1.92		* 30.86
	13	SEP16-75	RESTR	* 9.00		* 39.86
	14	SEP16-75				* 39.86
	15	SEP16-75	PHONE	* 1.20		* 41.06
	16					
	17					
	18					
	19					
	20					
	21					
	22					
	23					
	24					

LAST BALANCE IS AMOUNT DUE
BILLS ARE PAYABLE WHEN PRESENTED

Bunky Odom

SEPT. 13, 1975
Roosevelt Stadium
Jersey City, N.J.
$75,000/60/180,000
70/200,000
4,500 Sound, Lights, Piano
Muddy Waters - 6:00 - 6:45
Charlie Daniels 7:30 - 8:30
A.B.B. 9:00 - 1:00 A.M.
~~$750.00~~ Limos ~~500.00~~
* There's not but a 7 ft. stage

SEPTEMBER 18, 1975

THE SPECTRUM

PHILADELPHIA

After the Jersey City date, we stayed over in New York City for two off days before playing in New Haven, Connecticut, on September 15, 1975, again for John Scher. Then we had two more off days in New York City. Days off there always meant a big limo bill as both Gregg and Dickey each kept one on call virtually twenty-four hours a day. The owner of the limo service once told me his drivers had to take a few days off after Allman Brothers Band duty.

On September 18, 1975, we played the Spectrum in Philadelphia. The road-crew band, The Almost Brothers Band, was now often performing a short preshow set. It was a disguised sound check as the band itself, other than Chuck, Lamar, and Jaimoe, rarely showed up for a traditional sound check. Muddy Waters was the support act on several shows during this period. What a treat it was to have this living blues legend, whose songs were covered live and recorded by The Allman Brothers Band, perform at our concerts. I would sometimes use one of our limos to give him a ride to the airport after his set so he could get a flight home to Chicago that same night. The band earned a flat guarantee of $55,000 less that dreaded 1.5 percent city income tax withholding of $828.12.

SEPTEMBER 21, 1975

BOSTON GARDEN

BOSTON

We had another two days off before performing at Boston Garden for promoter Don Law on September 21, 1975. Muddy Waters was support again. The band earned a $50,000 guarantee plus an overage performance bonus of $5,373.40. For the month of September, we played nine cities in nine states, earning $404,447.12, an average of almost $45,000 per concert. It was an impressive take, but expenses and overhead with a lot of days off were extremely high. Profits for this tour would be much lower than normal.

OCTOBER 1975

VARIOUS

We opened up October 1975 with a successful, but not blockbuster, concert in Atlanta's Omni for promoter Alex Cooley. Jimmy Carter was our guest, and we agreed to do a benefit concert to kick-start his embryonic presidential campaign. A new law allowed certain donations, such as this, to receive matching funds from the government. The band earned a $40,000 guarantee in Atlanta plus an overage performance bonus of $3,646.25.

We then headed out West for one show in Arizona and five in California. I recall I was very angry with both Gregg and Dickey for what I considered unprofessional conduct on their part. One show in Bakersfield, California, for Bill Graham was an unmitigated financial disaster for both him and the band. It was a "90/10" deal, and our earnings were 90 percent of the net box office receipts, or just $933.45. Graham did have a successful show two nights later in Oakland. Also, about this time we started having to carry a chiropractor on the road to give Jaimoe daily adjustments for his chronic back pain and swelling. This was another big, but necessary, outflow of funds with the doctor's fees, travel, and lodging expenses. The average earnings for October were $26,000 per show, about half of normal earnings and way off peak earnings. The tires were getting low and the gas tank was half empty on the cash-earning juggernaut known as The Allman Brothers Band.

NOVEMBER 25, 1975

CIVIC CENTER

PROVIDENCE, RHODE ISLAND

We performed the benefit for Jimmy Carter on November 25, 1975, at the Civic Center in Providence, Rhode Island, promoted by Tony Ruffino, Larry Vaughn, and Don Law, with Grinderswitch opening. Neither the promoters nor The Allman Brothers Band took any remuneration. Attendance was just under ten thousand, and the net profit after sales taxes and building fees was approximately $60,000. Carter has said that $60,000 infusion of cash enabled him to go forward with his candidacy. Regardless of one's politics, he was a good and decent man who served, and continues to live, with dignity and honor.

The Secret Service did background checks on the entire band and crew. I'm sure that provided some interesting reading, but everyone was cleared to be around the candidate. When I thanked the Treasury Department for the courtesy and professionalism of their agents at the concert, they were astounded. No one had ever done that before.

PROVIDENCE CIVIC CENTER

ONE LASALLE SQUARE
PROVIDENCE, RHODE ISLAND 02903
401 - 331-0700

053

PERF. # ______

ATTRACTION Allman Bros.

PLAY DATES ______

DAY Tuesday DATE 11-25-75 TIME 8:00 PM

BOX OFFICE STATEMENT

WEATHER Clear ATTN: 9929

BOX COUNT	MANIFEST CAPACITY	FULL TICKETS	PRESS PASSES	SPECIAL RATES	TOTAL NOT SOLD AT FULL PRICE	SOLD	EST. PRICE	HOUSE RECEIPTS	CITY/STATE TAX RATE	CITY/STATE TAX AMOUNT	GOV'T TAX RATE	GOV'T TAX AMOUNT
	4000	2505			2505	1495	7.50	11,212.50	.40	598.00		
	14000	5343	531		5874	8126	6.50	52,819.00	.35	2844.10		
TOTALS	18000	7848	531		8379	9621		64031.50		3442.10		

Included in Gross:
Due to T. Ruffino – Ticketron – 5239.00
Due Civic Center 1007.50
from Carter Campaign
Deduct from settlement

ADVANCE/FRESH
TOTAL GROSS SALES TO DATE
TOTAL EARNED GROSS TO DATE
GROSS ADVANCE REMAINING

WE HEREBY CERTIFY THAT THE UNDERSIGNED HAVE PERSONALLY CHECKED THE ABOVE STATEMENT AND IT IS IN EVERY WAY CORRECT.

ADMISSIONS CONTROL MGR.
SHOW MANAGER

TOTAL GROSS $64,031.50
BALANCE FORWARD 60,589.40
GROSS TO DATE

TONY RUFFINO,

LARRY VAUGHN

& DON LAW

present

The Allman Brothers Band

SPECIAL GUEST

GRINDERSWITCH

IN A BENEFIT CONCERT FOR

Jimmy Carter For President

PROVIDENCE CIVIC CENTER; TUES., NOV. 25, 1975

NOVEMBER 27, 1975

MADISON SQUARE GARDEN

NEW YORK, NEW YORK

The Allman Brothers Band celebrated Thanksgiving in New York City at Madison Square Garden on Thursday November 27, 1975, with Grinderswitch opening. Tony Ruffino promoted, and the band received a $55,000 fee. Ruffino provided muted television sets on stage for the crew to follow the Georgia-Georgia Tech football game. Georgia won 42–26. We had one other show for Tony Ruffino on November 29, in Rochester, New York, earning a $30,000 guarantee and an overage performance bonus of $8,559.87.

In November, excluding the benefit, the band played seven shows in six states, grossing $257,413.36, or almost a $37,000 per show average. It was good, profitable, but not great business, and despite some highlights, band and crew morale was not improving.

DECEMBER 8, 1975

MEMORIAL AUDITORIUM

BUFFALO, NEW YORK

We kicked off December 1975 with a date in Springfield, Massachusetts, on December 1, followed by Buffalo, New York, at the Memorial Auditorium on December 8. It was promoted by Harvey Weinstein and Corky Burger, and we earned $45,000. Mr. Weinstein would go on to become a very powerful and successful movie producer in Hollywood. More recently, he has received notoriety for alleged sexual misconduct and was sentenced to a long term in prison. Attorney John Condon and his family were our guests at the concert for a purely social visit. We didn't know then that we would soon require his legal services again for perhaps the most serious legal misadventure yet.

DECEMBER 31, 1975

CIVIC CENTER

LAKELAND, FLORIDA

As always, New Year's Eve was a happy and lucrative payday for The Allman Brothers Band. It was an evening for great music shared among the band, crew, fans, friends, and family, including Cher. For the first time, we played the Civic Center in Lakeland, Florida. Grinderswitch opened, and it was a long, great show extending well past midnight. The band earned a $32,500 guarantee plus an overage performance bonus of $7,413.60. For the month, we played eight shows in seven states, grossing $256,580.40, with a per-show average of $32,000.

1975 had provided major disappointments for the band in record sales and concert earnings, with deepening creative and personal differences. The spirit and brotherhood that had always been our strong point were ebbing. Most of us were discouraged and disappointed, but I had high hopes for a rebound in the new year. I didn't really believe it, though, and it was not to be.

0021840
GENERAL ADMISSION
NEW YEAR'S EVE WITH
THE ALLMAN BROTHERS BAND
LAKELAND CIVIC CENTER
DEC'BR
31
1975
NO REFUNDS
Wed. Eve. at 8:00
Est. Pr. 7.69
St. Tax .31
TOTAL
$8.00
PRODUCED BY
CONCERTS WEST
& GULF ARTISTS
GLOBE TICKET CO. S260
LAKELAND CIVIC CENTER
ALLMAN BROS. BAND
DECEMBER
WED'DAY EVE.
GOOD ONLY
31
1975

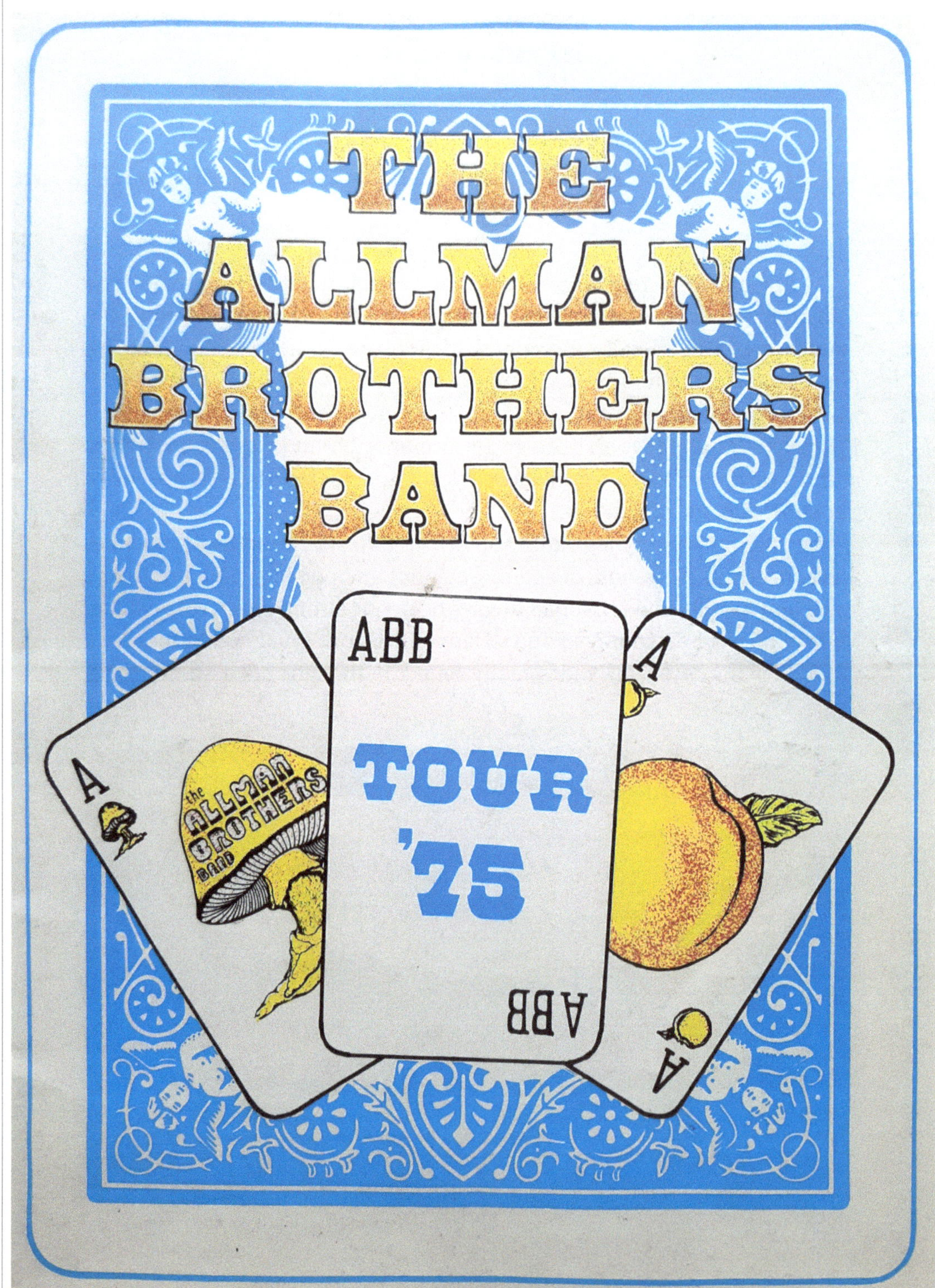
THE
ALLMAN
BROTHERS
BAND
ABB
TOUR
'75
ABB
A
A
the
ALLMAN
BROTHERS
BAND
A
A

1976

VARIOUS

There was even more expensive bad news afoot as we began the year 1976. We learned from reliable sources that the US Attorney's Office for the Middle District of Georgia had impaneled a grand jury regarding two separate investigations. One was related to so-called "Dixie Mafia" activities in the area, and the other centered on a local pharmacist involved in a prescription-drug and pharmaceutical-cocaine conspiracy. Our employee, John "Scooter" Herring, was a person of interest in both. Several others, including Gregg Allman and myself, were being investigated in the drug-conspiracy portion. Additionally, we also found out that national Republican Party interests, including the Nixon-appointed judge, might be interested in attempting to smear candidate Jimmy Carter for his relationship with manager Phil Walden and The Allman Brothers Band. Politics can be a very nasty business.

In early January, we flew to Texas for three dates in Fort Worth, Houston, and San Antonio. Gregg, Scooter, and I were ordered to appear before the grand jury the morning after San Antonio on a day off before we played Kansas City. This was an unduly harsh requirement, and we asked for a postponement since we had a full schedule for the entire month. Permission was denied under a threat of contempt of court by the presiding judge. This necessitated chartering a small jet to fly us back to Macon while the remainder of the band and crew flew on to Kansas City in the regular charter. We left late evening January 12, after the San Antonio concert, and would meet the others in Kansas City on January 14. Arriving in Macon in the early morning hours, we were unable to land due to heavy fog. We diverted to Atlanta, where we were also unable to land because of the fog. Finally, with fuel running low, we were able to land at the smaller Fulton County Airport through a small break in the fog and took limos to Macon. We were exhausted, irritated, and a little bit nervous. Attorney John Condon had arrived in Macon earlier and was there to meet us. He advised us to refuse to answer questions under our legal rights provided by the First, Fourth, Fifth, Sixth, and Ninth Amendments to the Constitution. A bullet was temporarily dodged, and we later flew on to Kansas City to make the date. Again, we were hit with a huge added

KEXL
INTRODUCES
THE
ALLMAN BROTHERS
BAND
LIVE! IN CONCERT!
MON. JAN. 12
SAN ANTONIO
ARENA
TICKETS:
$5.50, 6.50
RESERVED
PLUS S/C
TICKETS AVAILABLE AT:
JAM & JELLY GENERAL
STORE; ARENA BOX OFFICE;
FLIP-SIDE RECORDS; RAY-
MOND'S DRUGS IN AUSTIN.
SAN ANTONIO INFO: 828-6351

expense not in our budget. Destructive ramifications of this investigation were delayed but did not disappear.

I don't think the band ever fully understood the extent of our increasing expenses and decreasing revenues. Gregg, Dickey, and Butch continued their lavish lifestyles with no adjustments. In January 1976, we played nine dates in seven states, earning $244,653.93, an average of $27,000 per show. Most future bookings were put on hold because of our inability to get the terms necessary to maintain earnings at the level needed. The yellow caution light was blinking brightly. We would not play another paid concert until the last day of April.

MARCH 13, 1976

NASSAU COLISEUM

UNIONDALE, NEW YORK

Even in the midst of financial distress and personal and creative differences, The Allman Brothers Band would respond positively to requests for the donation of their services for benefit concerts. Prominent broadcaster and newsman Geraldo Rivera made a personal request for the band to headline a concert to benefit his charitable foundation One to One. The proceeds from the concert would benefit mentally challenged children. The Marshall Tucker Band also appeared. The concert was hugely successful, and many thousands of dollars were raised.

APRIL 30, 1976

KENTUCKY FAIR & EXPO CENTER

LOUISVILLE, KENTUCKY

We returned to work again on April 30, 1976, with a prime booking during Kentucky Derby week in Louisville, Kentucky. Other concerts during the week featured John Denver, Up with People, and Ray Stevens. A part of our concert was included on a Friday-night pre-Derby special of ABC's *Wide World of Sports* with Chris Schenkel and Howard Cosell. We had a great time partying with their crew, and we scored some complimentary tickets to the race. The concert earned the band a $50,000 guarantee and an overage performance bonus of $15,069.57. For a brief, fleeting moment, better times seemed to be back.

LOWE AVIATION COMPANY
MUNICIPAL AIRPORT
PHONE AREA 912 - 788-3491
P.O. BOX 4401
MACON, GA. 31208
SALES • SERVICE • PARTS • AIRCRAFT ENGINE & AIRFRAME
No. 49796 CUSTOMER'S ORDER NO. DATE 4-29 1976
NAME Allman Brothers Band
ADDRESS
SOLD BY CGC CASH C.O.D. CHARGE ON ACCT. MDSE. RET. PAID OUT

QTY	DESCRIPTION	PRICE	AMOUNT
	707 WA Fairchild		
460	Gal. Jet	.59	271 40
	PAID MAY - 6 1976		
	CHECK NO. 1256 $1300.43 Fed.		32 20
	TAX		8 14
	TOTAL		311 74

ALL CLAIMS AND RETURNED GOODS MUST BE ACCOMPANIED BY THIS BILL

No 9346 General Admission
KY. DERBY FESTIVAL – WAKY
SOUND SEVENTY – TRIGG BLACK PROD.
PRESENTS
ALLMAN BROTHERS BAND
APRIL 30 1976
FRIDAY AT 8:00 P.M.
FREEDOM HALL
KENTUCKY FAIR & EXPOSITION CENTER
LOUISVILLE, KENTUCKY
ADVANCE $7.50
NO REFUND-NO EXCHANGE–KY. SALES TAX INCL.
FRI. EVE.. APRIL 30 GOOD ONLY
GENERAL ADMISSION No 9346

Kentucky
Derby
Festival
'76

MAY 4, 1976

CIVIC CENTER

ROANOKE, VIRGINIA

After a so-so date in Knoxville, Tennessee, on May 2, 1976, we journeyed to Roanoke, Virginia, for a date at the Civic Center on Tuesday, May 4, 1976. We received a guarantee of $25,000 and the date was not financially successful for the promoter.

And, just like that, it was over. There were no more dates on the books to be fulfilled. After experiencing the highest of highs and the lowest of lows professionally and personally, The Allman Brothers Band would officially break up in June 1976. Scooter Herring's criminal indictment and Gregg Allman's subsequent testimony against him led to Gregg's temporary estrangement from his bandmates. Additionally, there was a creative malaise, my resignation in protest, financial problems, continuing drug and alcohol abuse, and many other factors which brought us to that moment. Almost immediately I became personal manager of Sea Level, a band comprised of Chuck Leavell, Jaimoe, Lamar Williams, and Jimmy Nalls. The band signed with Capricorn Records, began touring, and had a moderately successful run for several years before moving on to other projects. The other band members soon formed their own musical endeavors with limited success. The Allman Brothers Band story, though, was not over yet.

MEMORANDUM
4/13/76

TO: SCOOTER-information
WILLIAM- " "
BUNKY-
PAT- for contract action

RE: STAGE IN ROANOKE

Even after approving the building's stage, I had Phil Lashinsky go do a physical check of the stage and his report is that with the lighting, sound and equipment he recommends having Jerry Julian bring a stage.

His quote was 4'6", 80' x 40' for a net cost increase of $1800.00.

I offered to split it with him to allow $900.00, I am increasing the break by $1500.00 (60%= $900.00).

In addition he is adding another $500.00 of his own money to get Jerry Julian to bring the stage height up to 6 feet.

Lashinsky is very concerned about getting a good report. He remembers being"iced" out from 1973.

AFTERWORD

After the first breakup of The Allman Brothers Band in 1976, they would reform, break up again, and reform again, performing until 2014. As a tour manager and personal manager, I would be associated with Sea Level, The Gregg Allman Band, and others before becoming copersonal manager of The Allman Brothers Band Twentieth Anniversary Tour of 1989. With the second generation of sons and daughters now performing, the road still goes on forever.

Willie Perkins
Macon, Georgia
January 25, 2022

ACKNOWLEDGMENTS

I would like to thank Gus Arrendale and Springer Mountain Farms for their continued support and friendship. Thanks to Charlie Oliver and the Charlie Oliver Collection for access to and use of their memorabilia collection and to Jack Weston for his brilliant photo editing and enhancement. All images are courtesy of the Charlie Oliver Collection unless otherwise noted. Thanks to Bunky Odom and Albert Teebagy for their recollections. Thanks to Bill Walsh for the photo of Duane Allman and Little Richard. Thanks to The Allman Brothers Band members and road crew for giving me a lifetime of wonderful memories and for their faith and trust in me. And, as always, a very special thanks to the entire staff of Mercer University Press for their support and friendship through the years.

And thanks to Billy Bob Thornton for inspiration.

MUSIC AND THE AMERICAN SOUTH

Jack† and Olivia Solomon†, *Honey in the Rock: The Ruby Pickens Tartt Collection of Religious Folk Songs from Sumter County, Alabama*

Zell Miller,† *They Heard Georgia Singing*

David Fillingim,† *Redneck Liberation: Country Music as Theology*

Willie Perkins, *No Saints, No Saviors: My Years with the Allman Brothers Band*

Anathalee G. Sandlin, *A Never-Ending Groove: Johnny Sandlin's Musical Odyssey*

Michael P. Graves and David Fillingim,† ed., *More Than Precious Memories: The Rhetoric of Southern Gospel Music*

Michael Buffalo Smith,† *Prisoner of Southern Rock: A Memoir*, with a Foreword by Billy Bob Thornton

Michael Buffalo Smith,† *Rebel Yell: An Oral History of Southern Rock*, with a Foreword by Alan Walden

Willie Perkins and Jack Weston, *The Allman Brothers Band Classic Memorabilia, 1969–1976*, with a Foreword by Galadrielle Allman

Michael Buffalo Smith,† *Capricorn Rising: Conversations in Southern Rock*, with a Foreword by Willie Perkins

Michael Buffalo Smith,† *From Macon to Jacksonville: More Conversations in Southern Rock*, with a Foreword by Charlie Starr

Michael Buffalo Smith,† *The Road Goes on Forever: Fifty Years of The Allman Brothers Band Music (1969–2019)*, with a Foreword Chuck Leavell

Doug Kershaw, *The Ragin' Cajun: Memoir of a Louisiana Man*, with Cathie Pelletier

Don Reid, *The Music of The Statler Brothers: An Anthology*, with a Foreword by Bill and Gloria Gaither

Paul Hornsby, *Fix it in the Mix: A Memoir*, with Michael Buffalo Smith†

Ben Wynne, *Something in the Water: A History of Music in Macon, Georgia, 1823–1980*

Bill Thames, *Paper, Scissors, Rock-N-Roll: Ringo, Duane, & Me*